D1281055

XXX

*FIRE: A WAR
THAT NEVER ENDS*

XXXXXXXXXXXXXXXXXXXXXXXXXXXXXXXXXXXXXXXXXXXXXXXXXXXXXXXXXXXXXXXXXXX

Photo by Larry Rand, Ladder 153 Auxiliary. (c. 1977)

XXX

ABOUT THE AUTHOR

Ernie DiMaria was appointed to the New York City Fire Department in November of 1968. After six weeks of training he was assigned to one of the busiest firehouses in the city.

The high fire incidence of the '60s continued into the '70s with record breaking numbers of arson fires as well as false alarms. Adding to the strife of the times was a "fiscal crisis" in 1975 that bred layoffs of firefighters, cops and other city workers and the cancellation of hiring and promotional exams.

Eventually (in August 1979), he managed to get promoted to lieutenant and served until voluntary retirement in 1989.

During his career he received four meritorious awards in addition to New York State certifications as EMT and Fire Service Instructor.

His son, Richie, is a U.S. Naval Officer.

XXXXXXXXXXXXXXXXXXXXXXXXXXXXXXXXXXXXXXXXXXXXXXXXXXXXXXXXXXXXXXXXX

XX

Victor Cole
1992

XXXXXXXXXXXXXXXXXXXXXXXXXXXXXXXXXXXXXXXXXXXXXXXXXXXXXXXXXXXXXXXXXXXXXXXXXXXXXX

XXX

"FIRE: A WAR THAT NEVER ENDS"

An introspective account of the fire that killed six New York City firemen on August 2, 1978.

by Ernie DiMaria

Edited by Victor Cole

SUNSET *Bookstore*
P.O. Box 81024
Las Vegas, NV 89180

XXXXXXXXXXXXXXXXXXXXXXXXXXXXXXXXXXXXXXXXXXXXXXXXXXXXXXXXXXXXXXXXX

XX

Front cover:

> "Brothers" by Dave Hirsch
> (c) 1977

Back cover:
> UFA/UFOA Firemen's Medal of Supreme Sacrifice
> Photo courtesy of Louise O'Connor

> "Opening Up" by J. Capriano
> (c) 1980 New York Firefighters Burn Center Foundation

Copyright (c) 1993 by Ernest DiMaria
All rights reserved. No part of this book may be
reproduced by any means whatsoever without written
permission from the publisher, except for brief
quotations in a review.
Applicable fees for permission to use copyrighted
material in this book were paid by author.

Manufactured in the United States of America.

Published by: SUNSET *Bookstore*
                 P.O. Box 81024
                 Las Vegas, NV 89180

Library of Congress Catalog Card Number: 93-84762

Publisher's Cataloging in Publication Data

DiMaria, Ernest F., 1946-
FIRE: A War That Never Ends / by Ernie DiMaria
1.Autobiographical
Includes bibliography. p.184
Includes index.
1.Firefighters-New York, NY
2.Rescue Work Stress-psychological aspects
3.History-FDNY

ISBN: 0-9637296-1-6 (hardcover)

XXXXXXXXXXXXXXXXXXXXXXXXXXXXXXXXXXXXXXXXXXXXXXXXXXXXXXXXXXXXXXXXXXXX

XXX

TO RICHIE,

MY ETERNAL SOURCE OF

PRIDE AND JOY!

XXX

*"The only true gift is
a portion of thyself."*

Ralph Waldo Emerson

XXXXXXXXXXXXXXXXXXXXXXXXXXXXXXXXXXXXXXXXXXXXXXXXXXXXXXXXXXXXXXXXX

XXX

CONTENTS

PAGE

XXXXXXXXXXXXXXXXXXXXXXXXXXXXXXXXXXXXXXXXXXXXXXXXXXXXXXXXXXXXXXXXX

"Nice Job ... Kid" by John Goss

Three words that are as good as an official medal.

XXXXXXXXXXXXXXXXXXXXXXXXXXXXXXXXXXXXXXXXXXXXXXXXXXXXXXXXXXXXXXXX

XX

FOREWORD

Ernie DiMaria hit the bullseye when he said, "Every FDNY member at the fire scene that day (8/2/78) has a story inside him."

Let me tell you of my experience on Feb. 4, 1989:
John Devaney, a firefighter I never met, lost his life in the performance of duty the day before. John Devaney did not exhaust himself to the point of having a heart attack. He died a violent, tragic, sudden death, as did the six men at the Waldbaum fire.

As then-Captains Representative for the *Uniformed Fire Officers Association, Local 854, I responded to Ladder Company 131, Devaney's assigned unit, to offer my assistance, sympathy, support and advice.

I left the firehouse, which is located in the Red Hook section of Brooklyn, and headed home to my apartment in Bay Ridge. About 20 blocks away on Fourth Avenue, I stopped for a red light. Then it happened; ten and a half years later, as Ernie did on August 2, 1978, I cried a tearful, sobbing, uncontrollable cry.

*UFOA, International Association of Fire Fighters (IAFF), AFL-CIO

XXXXXXXXXXXXXXXXXXXXXXXXXXXXXXXXXXXXXXXXXXXXXXXXXXXXXXXXXXXXXXXXXXXX

I realized, while waiting for the red light, that I had just seen the faces of Ernie DiMaria, Harry Latting, Joe Tufano, Walter Brett and every other firefighter involved in the Waldbaum fire, in the quarters of Ladder Company 131. The unbelieving, compassionate, sympathetic, helpless, lost soul look of the survivors of the war that never ends.

Yes Ernie, "Every member at the fire scene that day has a story inside him." You finally told yours and did it well. Thanks, Brother!

Edward J. Smith
Retired Capt., FDNY
Former Pres., UFOA

XXX

ACKNOWLEDGMENTS TO:

VICTOR COLE, my editor,
for his expertise and encouragement to hang in there.

PATRICIA GONZALEZ,
for her technical assistance and advice.

HERB EYSSER,
for historical data on the NYC Firemen's Monument.

FRANK J. MIALE,
for introducing me to a word processor.

JEFFREY T. MITCHELL, Ph.D.,
for his pioneering work on Critical Incident Stress
Debriefing for the Emergency Services.

The FDNY officers and senior members who served as my
role models and whose guidance, experience and wisdom
cannot be measured.

* * * * * * AND * * * * * *

A SPECIAL ACKNOWLEDGMENT

*To Louise O'Connor, whose unsolicited support for
this project may require another 15 years to find
the proper words of appreciation.*

XXXXXXXXXXXXXXXXXXXXXXXXXXXXXXXXXXXXXXXXXXXXXXXXXXXXXXXXXXXXXXXXX

"Opening Up" by J. Capriano

Copyright 1980 New York Firefighters Burn Center Foundation

XXXXXXXXXXXXXXXXXXXXXXXXXXXXXXXXXXXXXXXXXXXXXXXXXXXXXXXXXXXXXXXXXXXX

XX

INTRODUCTION

On the morning of August 2, 1978, in Brooklyn, New York, a fire was reported in a supermarket that was undergoing some renovation. Approximately one half hour later, the New York City Fire Department suffered its third worst disaster ever.

Without the usual warning signs that firefighters are trained to look for, the roof of the building collapsed. The increased exposure to air intensified the fire more than tenfold and the building literally swallowed up 12 men, allowing only six to escape or be rescued.

At this point, let me tell you what this book is not; it is ***not*** a textbook on building construction or the art of firefighting. Nor is it an investigative report on every aspect of the supermarket fire. Also, don't expect me to take you literarily through the heat, smoke and flames.

The main purpose of this story is to emphasize the frustration and helplessness from the rescuer's viewpoint, when the battle to save a life is lost. After a fatal fire, a firefighter wonders what else could have been done to prevent the loss of life, and if the victim was a firefighter, also realizes how easily it could have been him or her. This realization is the basis of the kinship, if you will, of firefighters everywhere.

XXXXXXXXXXXXXXXXXXXXXXXXXXXXXXXXXXXXXXXXXXXXXXXXXXXXXXXXXXXXXXXXXX

XXX

Firefighters have no desire to be dead heroes. They take the risks and if they lose, so be it; but they do not give their lives away as if in some barter system. What they give is a portion of themselves to their communities and to mankind itself. Until we evolve sufficiently to master control of fire and prevent arson, lives and property will be lost and rescuers will die trying to save them. In return for their service, some firefighters receive a modest paycheck, while the vast majority who are volunteers get no salary. Hopefully, all of them get a measure of respect from the society they serve.

I would guess that the desire to write about my experience started out as a sort of self-help therapy; to work my thoughts and feelings out through writing. Not an easy task when you've been shocked and confused. The decision to write about it did not come until February 1982, but I didn't start making written notes until the summer of '87. Talk about writer's block!

At last I have reached my goal of presenting my story, together with factual data and actual newspaper coverage. Every FDNY member at the fire scene that day has a story inside him; this is just one of them. I hope to convey to the reader my observations and feelings as they occurred; not as a reporter or historian, but as a firefighter humbled by the awesome power of fate.

Ideally, all those affected (FDNY personnel, friends and relatives of the deceased and injured), could have been inter- viewed and quoted in order to document thoroughly what trans-

XXXXXXXXXXXXXXXXXXXXXXXXXXXXXXXXXXXXXXXXXXXXXXXXXXXXXXXXXXXXXXXXX

pired as they saw it and how it affected them. Such a task would have bcen difficult and I preferred not to risk "opening closed wounds," as it were; including my own. It was hard enough reliving that week in 1978 each time I found it necessary to proofread.

Regarding documentation, which is included in Part 4, the newspapers did an excellent job recording this major event in the history of the New York City Fire Department. The compilation of these sources may serve as a ready reference to satisfy any historical interest.

Another reason for this book is to encourage the use of Critical Incident Stress De-Briefing (CISD) programs for all emergency rescue personnel, not only the fire service. Leaders at all levels of government and their department chiefs (police, fire, paramedics, EMTs, Coast Guard. etc.) should support such programs. Those who do not would add a new dimension to the term, "expendable."

Last, and most important, I sincerely hope we continue to remember all who have been taken from us in defense of life, and pray that the burden of grief upon their families be somehow lightened.

* * * * * *

*When there is nothing you can do,
nothing is ever enough.*

XXXXXXXXXXXXXXXXXXXXXXXXXXXXXXXXXXXXXXXXXXXXXXXXXXXXXXXXXXXXXX

ENGINE Co. 30 — MANHATTAN
Organized: October 25, 1865
Disbanded: April 1, 1959

The New York City Fire Museum is presently located
in Engine Co. 30's old quarters at 278 Spring Street

Photo courtesy of Herb Eysser

xxxxxxxxxxxxxxxxxxxxxxxxxxxxxxxxxxxxxxxxxxxxxxxxxxxxxxxxxxxxxxxxxxx

xxxxxxxxxxxxxxxxxxxxxxxxxxxxxxxxxxxxxxxxxxxxxxxxxxxxxxxxxxxxxxxxxxxxx

During the author's 20 years in the FDNY, there were 93 line-of-duty deaths.

PART 1

"SOME FACTS AND FIGURES"

Until August 2nd, the year 1978 was relatively good for the New York City Fire Department, which lost only one firefighter on July 13th. Since the *FDNY was organized in 1865, it has averaged about six line-of-duty deaths annually. Although it may sound morbid, losing only one firefighter in seven months is "relatively good," when you consider the statistics. While statistics have their place, there is nothing good (relatively or otherwise) about six wives losing their husbands and 18 children losing their fathers.

*Official abbreviation for Fire Department of New York (City)

xxxxxxxxxxxxxxxxxxxxxxxxxxxxxxxxxxxxxxxxxxxxxxxxxxxxxxxxxxxxxxxxxxxxx

Besides leaving families and friends in grief, these men left thousands of co-workers, in this most unique of all professions, to think hard about what they do for a living and to study what happened and how it might have been prevented.

The focus of study was placed on the method of construction known as "truss," which is used to support the weight of floors, roofs, bridges, etc. Without going into detail, a truss support is structurally strong but may fail quickly and suddenly when exposed to fire.

Quite reasonably you may ask, "Why do they build something with such a potential for danger?" As I stated in the Introduction, this is not a textbook or an investigative report, and I certainly do not wish to debate or attack the construction industry or municipal building codes.

This writer presumes that professionals and experts are not irresponsible and accordingly, cooperate with each other when inquiries are made. When it comes to public safety, it should be no other way. Enough said!

Following are selected data from the fire report and some stats on fire-related collapse:

xxx

Date:	August 2, 1978
Time reported:	0839 hours (8:39 a.m.)
Address:	Waldbaums Supermarket 2892 Ocean Ave. Brooklyn, New York
Construction:	1 story brick, 100' x 150'
Duration:	16 hours and 8 minutes (under control at 1229 hours)
Alarm Box #:	44-3300 (4th alarm)
Casualties:	6 firefighters killed, 31 injured (No civilian casualties)

FDNY units utilized at incident:

22 Engines	Ambulance No. 2
1 Squad	Field Communications Unit
9 Ladders	Mask Service Unit
4 Rescue Companies	Fire Marshal
3 Battalions	FDNY Chaplains
2 Divisions (D.15 for relief)	

Command Personnel: Augustus Beekman,   Fire Commissioner
                     Francis Cruthers,   Chief of Department
                     Homer G. Bishop,   Brooklyn Borough
                                          Commander

Deceased Members:

Rank	Name	Unit	Badge
Lieut.	James E. Cutillo	Batt. 33	638
Fr. 1st Gr.	Charles S. Bouton	L.156	3162
Fr. 4th Gr.	William O'Connor	L.156	3144
Fr. 1st Gr	James P. McManus	L.153	7409
Fr. 1st Gr	George Rice	L.153	5895
Fr. 1st Gr	Harold F. Hastings	Batt. 42	11177

xxxxxxxxxxxxxxxxxxxxxxxxxxxxxxxxxxxxxxxxxxxxxxxxxxxxxxxxxxxxxxxxxxxx

In terms of multiple firefighter fatalities in a single collapse incident, the worst documented were as follows:

Reference: "Collapse of Burning Buildings,"
              by Vincent Dunn, Deputy Chief, FDNY

DATE	PLACE	KILLED	TYPE OF COLLAPSE
1910	Chicago	21	Stockyard building
1910	Philadelphia	14	Leather factory
1941	Brockton, Mass	13	Steel truss roof of movie theater
10/17/66	New York City (Manhattan)	12	Masonry floor supported by wood beams, into burning cellar.
6/17/72	Boston	9	Hotel (floors and walls)
4/4/56	New York City (Bronx)	6	*Parapet wall supporting a marquee.
10/27/62	New York City (Queens)	6	*Wall of soap factory.
8/2/78	New York City (Brooklyn)	6	Wood truss roof of a supermarket.

It is hoped that these men died swiftly and painlessly, but more than likely they were burned or asphyxiated after being crushed or trapped beneath heavy debris.

As in these cases, a collapse may occur after the fire is declared under control.

XXXXXXXXXXXXXXXXXXXXXXXXXXXXXXXXXXXXXXXXXXXXXXXXXXXXXXXXXXXXXXX

During the 30 years 1956-1986, 46 FDNY members were killed by fire-related collapse of a floor, wall, roof, or pier.

In his book, Deputy Chief Dunn lists the names of all 46 members. The following breakdown by rank shows no discrimination by the grim reaper:

   1 Deputy Chief

   2 Battalion Chiefs

   3 Captains

   7 Lieutenants

  33 Firefighters

There are survivors of fire-related collapses, but virtually all of them remain forever scarred, either physically, emotionally, or both.

*   *   *

Note: *The worst loss of firefighters sustained by*
              FDNY and not attributed to a collapse was
              the Ritz Hotel fire of August 1, 1932.
              Seven members perished at that fire.

xxxxxxxxxxxxxxxxxxxxxxxxxxxxxxxxxxxxxxxxxxxxxxxxxxxxxxxxxxxxxxxxxx

"Moving In" by J. Capriano

Copyright 1984 New York Firefighters Burn Center Foundation

xxxxxxxxxxxxxxxxxxxxxxxxxxxxxxxxxxxxxxxxxxxxxxxxxxxxxxxxxxxxxxxxxxxxxxxx

XX

"There are No Safe (Fire) Houses"
Pete Hamill
Daily News, 8/4/78

PART 2

"THROUGH MY EYES"

Many thousands of people have experienced the pain of loss due to fire's merciless destruction of a home, a business, or a life; and this pain should not be trivialized. It is the firefighter, however, who is subject to a unique sense of helplessness, because despite his courage, training, and desire to save and protect, lives are still lost.

When the loss is a brother firefighter, that sense of helplessness is magnified, and the task of dealing with it is compounded. When six firefighters are lost, it can make you speechless ... which is one reason it took so long to get this out and on paper.

XXXXXXXXXXXXXXXXXXXXXXXXXXXXXXXXXXXXXXXXXXXXXXXXXXXXXXXXXXXXXX

TRIGGERED MEMORIES

February 4, 1988: It was more than nine years since the fire, but it seemed like just the other day, especially whenever I passed by the building. Today, while stopped for the traffic light at Ocean Avenue and Avenue Y, I glanced at the south wall of the building as I had done countless times before. But this time something was different, and before the light changed, I became aware of what it was.

You see, on the day of the fire, the brick wall was breached in a rescue attempt, and then served as an exit for the bodies of the dead firefighters. Later on, the newly replaced bricks contrasted with the existing wall, very much like scar tissue after a skin laceration has healed.

"What was different now?" I asked myself. There was an increased accumulation of graffiti, but that wasn't it. Then I noticed, amid the graffiti, that time had weathered the new bricks, which made the repair almost unnoticeable.

So that was it! Weatherbeaten, faded bricks! Faded bricks, like faded memories. "Somewhere," I thought, "there is a correlation."

xxxxxxxxxxxxxxxxxxxxxxxxxxxxxxxxxxxxxxxxxxxxxxxxxxxxxxxxxxxxxxxxx

"Someday," I also thought, "I'm going to write a book!"

GETTING BAD NEWS

August 2, 1978: Today would have been my first day back to work after some vacation leave, but the captain had changed my group assignment in order to cover a chauffeur's vacation spot. So, I wasn't scheduled to work until the following night.

At about 10 a.m., the phone rang. After saying hello, I heard, "Thank God, you're safe!" It was my mother. She had just heard a report of a fire and building collapse in the Sheepshead Bay section of Brooklyn, and that some firemen were reported missing. She correctly presumed my fire company, Ladder 153, was there; hence the phone call. I told her I would check it out and call her back.

I called the Brooklyn dispatcher, and was given the location of the fire and that the units were still operating. I knew I had to help urgently in whatever way I could, but I also had to find a way to get there fast. Mindful of the requirement that members volunteering for duty be equipped with fire gear, I had to stop at the firehouse first.

XX

Via the Belt Parkway, Sheepshead Bay was less than 15 minutes away from Bay Ridge. But two months before, I had sold my '71 Buick because money was tight. The divorce in 1976 had cut my take home pay in half, but that's another story. However, I still had my motorcycle and quickly figured out what to do.

My parents resided about six blocks from the firehouse, so I asked them to meet me there and drive me to the fire. Still worried about my safety, my mother asked, "Do you have to go?" I was somewhat angry but more annoyed because she didn't understand that I couldn't just stay home and do nothing. I said, "Just meet me there!" and hung up the phone.

On the Belt Parkway, I fought back some tears, wondering if it was already too late to help in the rescue effort. I recalled going to a fire scene two and a half years before to volunteer at another collapse. I learned of that fire while on duty, as it was announced via the Voice Alarm in the middle of a January night tour. (1/7/76)

The Voice Alarm is a two-way loudspeaker system in every firehouse that is a direct link with the Borough Communications Office. It replaced the old

XXXXXXXXXXXXXXXXXXXXXXXXXXXXXXXXXXXXXXXXXXXXXXXXXXXXXXXXXXXXXXX

telegraph system, which required counting of bell signals by the *housewatchman. It also serves as a backup to the Computer Assisted Dispatch System [CADS], better known as the teleprinter.

I monitored the Department radio as the fire progressed to a 5th alarm. That fire, in an A & P supermarket, was in South Brooklyn, well out of Ladder 153's response area. I never knew why it was named "South Brooklyn," because geographically it is north. Surely there is a historical explanation, but I have never bothered to research it.

When the night tour ended that cold January morning, many of us went there because two firefighters were still missing and trapped in the cellar, due to the collapse of the first floor.

When I got there, Atlantic Avenue was a sea of helmets and turnout coats. The fire was under control and the last two men were found, but not soon enough for one of them. All the top brass was there, and TV cameras (including a helicopter for aerial shots) and reporters hovered to cover the story of the fire that claimed the life of Firefighter Charles Sanchez of Ladder 131.

*One word in FDNY terminology

XXXXXXXXXXXXXXXXXXXXXXXXXXXXXXXXXXXXXXXXXXXXXXXXXXXXXXXXXXXXXXXXXX

I never met Sanchez, but I know we took the same entrance exams back in 1968. He must have scored high, because he was in the first Probationary Class off that list.

I later learned that there were originally 12 members trapped in the cellar. I can only imagine the horror in the minds of the chief officers and senior members who were well aware of the 23rd Street fire in 1966, when a floor collapse took the lives of 12 of our bravest. How could fate allow this to happen twice in less than ten years?

Today (this time a hot summer day), I feared a similar outcome, compounded by the fact that I might know the victim (or victims) personally.

AT THE FIREHOUSE

I parked the motorcycle in the narrow alley alongside the firehouse. As I entered, Firefighter Bill Steen (Engine 254) was just leaving with his fire gear and on his way to the fire. Not wanting to hold him up, I didn't ask him to wait for me. Besides, my parents were already there, waiting in their car. Signaling that I would be right out, I went in to get my stuff.

XXXXXXXXXXXXXXXXXXXXXXXXXXXXXXXXXXXXXXXXXXXXXXXXXXXXXXXXXXXXXXXXXX

Inside, there were two relocated units assigned to respond to any subsequent alarm normally covered by Ladder 153 and Engine 254. This is a standard procedure during extended operations, to help maintain fire protection in the area. One of the units (Ladder 168), was, coincidentally, under the command of Lieutenant Massucci, a member of Ladder 153 until his promotion.

It was eerily quiet but I overheard something about the number six. The radio signal 10-45 (for fire victims) was not yet transmitted, but if anybody knew there were casualties, they weren't talking. Without asking, I picked up my gear and my dad took me to the fire scene. With the streets blocked and congested, I got out of the car about a block away, while he looked for a parking space.

ON THE SCENE

On Avenue Y, opposite the breached wall, I saw Engine 254's rig, with *MPO Phil Ruvolo by the controls. Although he was on the day tour relief crew, he looked like hell. Off-duty member Lieutenant McEnaney was standing next to him.

*Motor Pump Operator a/k/a Engine Company Chauffeur [ECC

McEnaney took me aside and told me the names of the six fatalities, and that Terry Campbell (L.153) was taken to the Burn Center. One of the victims, *Probationary Firefighter William O'Connor (L.156), was Phil's nephew. In a feeble attempt to comfort him, I put my hand on his shoulder for a moment and then went to the hole in the wall.

An ambulance was backed up onto the sidewalk to receive the body bags as they were carried from the building, passing from brother to brother. Dozens of hands worked with a diligent reverence until each body was taken away. I helped carry two of the bodies. I don't know which two, not that it matters. Meanwhile, more members were crowding around to help, so I stepped aside.

Just then, somebody told me my mom was looking for me. I saw her and my dad at the fire line and walked over to them. When I opened my mouth to speak, nothing came out. I managed to blurt out, "Six of them!" Then, in front of all those bystanders and in front of my mother, I cried. A tearful, sobbing, uncontrollable cry. She hugged me, and I felt somewhat embarrassed because of the staring bystanders.

*Member with less than one year service a/k/a "probie"

XXXXXXXXXXXXXXXXXXXXXXXXXXXXXXXXXXXXXXXXXXXXXXXXXXXXXXXXXXXXXX

I removed my turnout coat on that hot August day, and my blue T-shirt was soaked with sweat. An EMT (Emergency Medical Technician) holding a bottle of water offered to pour it on me to cool off. I tried to tell him to see to the on-duty members, but I still couldn't talk, so I just nodded a "No, thank you!"

After the dead and injured members were taken away, the day crew (L. 153) started to get ready to return to the firehouse, leaving the *overhauling to other relief units. Firefighter Vito Mattia of Ladder 153, came out of the fire building and told me, "I feel exhausted! I didn't do anything but I feel exhausted!" Then he asked me, "A chest pain could just be from stress, right?"

I replied, "Yeah, but EMS (Emergency Medical Services) is still here and they could check you out." But he said, "Nah, it's probably just stress! Yeah, that's it, only stress!" So much for a medical discussion between two firefighters.

*Generally, all related duties required after a fire is under control, including but not limited to, searching for hidden pockets of fire and wetting down smoldering debris. Usually takes considerably more time than extinguishment of the fire itself.

XXXXXXXXXXXXXXXXXXXXXXXXXXXXXXXXXXXXXXXXXXXXXXXXXXXXXXXXXXXXXXXXX

XX

Vito was on duty only about three hours in a relief capacity. With six men dead and 31 injured, he may have felt he had no right to feel ill. "Only stress!" he said. I should have dragged him by the collar to the ambulance. Well, at least I would have tried; we both stand over six feet tall. Besides, he was senior to me and it would have shown a lack of respect.

NOTE: Of four other members who complained of chest pains, three were hospitalized. One had suffered a heart attack.

According to the NFPA (National Fire Protection Association), physical stress (heart attack) is the number one cause of firefighter deaths.

RETURN TO QUARTERS

Drove back to the firehouse and told my parents to go home and I'd see them later. By the curb in front of quarters stood Ann Consalvo and a friend, I presumed, who accompanied her. Her husband, Augie, was assigned to Engine 254. I also thought she was standing outside because she didn't know anybody with the relocated companies. Perhaps she didn't want to invade the "domain" of the firehouse on this dark day.

XXXXXXXXXXXXXXXXXXXXXXXXXXXXXXXXXXXXXXXXXXXXXXXXXXXXXXXXXXXXXXXXXX

After recognizing me, she didn't have to speak; her eyes were asking me if her husband was all right. I assured her that he was OK and that he would be returning soon with the rest of the unit. She stayed outside to wait for him.

Inside the firehouse the pay phone was ringing, so I went in to answer it. The caller identified himself as a retired member. He was calling to advise us that Carole Rice (wife of George Rice) was driving to the fire scene. She did not know that George was killed, but he should have been home after getting off duty. Presumably, the news reports were enough to make her run to him.

The six 10-45s (*code 1) were transmitted via the Department radio at 10:52 a.m. Now that it was official, the news media undoubtedly reported it shortly thereafter. However, they may not report the names until after the families are notified.

I didn't know if the caller was aware that George was already gone, but he didn't ask me, either. He just wanted to be sure that a chaplain would be at the fire scene when Carole got there. I told him I'd take care of it.

*Fire victim deceased

XXXXXXXXXXXXXXXXXXXXXXXXXXXXXXXXXXXXXXXXXXXXXXXXXXXXXXXXXXXXXXX

XX

I knew the phone call was legitimate because we worked in the same firehouse in Bedford-Stuyvesant, and I recognized his voice. He was assigned to Engine 209 when I was a probie in Ladder 102. I didn't tell him who I was, because I wasn't in the mood to talk about old times.

As soon as I hung up I called the dispatcher's office, explained the situation, and asked to have a chaplain waiting for her. I don't know if the request was granted, because all the chaplains were probably getting ready to visit the families for official notification.

According to a subsequent news article, (p. 73) Carole was referred to Fire Commissioner Beekman at the scene by Firefighter Kenney of Tower Ladder 159. I'm sure glad I wasn't in the Commissioner's shoes that day!

As I hung up the phone, Engine 254 had just returned and parked across the street, in front of quarters. As the men dismounted the rig, a former member of Ladder 153, Joe Tufano, had just arrived and walked up to Lieutenant Smith to ask who the victims were. Tears welled up in Smith's eyes. As he shook his head and barely said, "I can't!" he looked at me as if to ask that I speak for him.

XXXXXXXXXXXXXXXXXXXXXXXXXXXXXXXXXXXXXXXXXXXXXXXXXXXXXXXXXXXXXXXX

I told Joe the names and he became distraught. I can only imagine the myriad feelings he had just then. Apparently, he realized that he might have been on that roof if he had not transferred out; perhaps he was sorry he had transferred; perhaps he was just as dumbfounded as most of us.

Joe was junior to me, an energetic type, always cooperative and willing to learn. Although he liked working in Ladder 153, he wanted to see more action, so he transferred to a busier unit. Later on, he got into one of the Rescue Companies to be among the "best of the best."

Lieutenant Edward Smith was assigned to Ladder 153, but worked the night tour in Engine 254 for Lieutenant Walter Brett in a mutual exchange of tours. Just recently, Ed (now Captain Smith) told me that Walter (now Battalion Chief Brett) had gone to the fire scene and, upon seeing Ed, had an indescribable expression of relief. If Smith was killed by the fire, Brett surely would have thought he died in his place; mistakenly perhaps, but nonetheless an unenviable position.

Ladder 153 returned to quarters and, as usual after a fire, most members gathered in the back room. At the rear of the apparatus floor, I saw two pairs of shoes where McManus and Rice always donned their fire boots. I didn't pick them up.

xxxxxxxxxxxxxxxxxxxxxxxxxxxxxxxxxxxxxxxxxxxxxxxxxxxxxxxxxxxxxxxxxxxxx

In the back room was an incredible blanket of sadness. I felt I needed a drink. I walked to the nearest liquor store, bought a bottle of scotch, and brought it into the firehouse. I poured myself a short one and placed the bottle on the table. It was the only time that I truly didn't care about the Regulations.

Anyway, both companies were placed out of service for the remainder of the day by Chief of Department Francis Cruthers. A kind gesture, but basically the extent of authorized stress reduction at that time. And certainly not meant to condone drinking in the firehouse.

I remember Lieutenant Ray Jones (L.153) saying, "I think I'll get started on the paperwork!" as he went up to the office. Because I had studied for promotion, I knew what the paperwork entailed and did not envy his task.

After pouring some more scotch, I went upstairs to see Lieut. Jones. I showed it to him and asked, "Do you want some of this?" He took it and said, "Thanks!" Then he handed me the empty glass.

XXXXXXXXXXXXXXXXXXXXXXXXXXXXXXXXXXXXXXXXXXXXXXXXXXXXXXXXXXXXXXX

Now, there is no way to justify bringing liquor into the firehouse; it was wrong! Furthermore, the latest studies show that alcohol is not recommended in critical incident stress situations. Actually, I didn't see anyone else touch the bottle.

I went back downstairs and suddenly, it seemed, there was nothing else for me to do and I felt like going home. As I backed my motorcycle out from the side of the firehouse, Augie Consalvo came out and asked me if I was all right. I don't know why he did, except that maybe I didn't look so good. I told him I was OK and then said, "I'll see ya!"

Walking home after garaging the motorcycle, I saw people going about their business and wondered if they knew about the fire; and if they did know, I wondered if they cared. Working in New York City, you don't expect too much thanks or recognition from the general public. But today I almost wanted to pin my badge on my chest and say, "Hey, look at me! I'm one of those guys who could have been killed today protecting people like you!"

I felt angry at that moment. I didn't know it then, but all I needed was someone to say, "I'm sorry about what happened to your buddies."

XXXXXXXXXXXXXXXXXXXXXXXXXXXXXXXXXXXXXXXXXXXXXXXXXXXXXXXXXXXXXXXX

Thankfully, there are many people who do appreciate us and pray for our safety. At times, elderly women have been seen making the sign of the cross as a fire truck passed by, presumably for us as well as those in peril.

Months, perhaps years later, I would hear a line from the TV show, "McCloud," in which Dennis Weaver said, "There are too many tragedies in New York City to get shook up over each one!"

How sad, but true. Living (and surviving) in the Big Apple is hard enough without taking the time to be empathetic.

Not wanting to stay alone that night, I called a friend who lived in Manhattan and asked if I could stay over.

I took the subway.

* * *

THE NEW YORK FIREFIGHTERS BURN CENTER
FOUNDATION

PREVENTION * CARE * RESEARCH

xxxxxxxxxxxxxxxxxxxxxxxxxxxxxxxxxxxxxxxxxxxxxxxxxxxxxxxxxxxxxxxxxxxxxxx

XX

AT THE BURN CENTER

August 3, 1978: That morning my friend had gone to work and I let myself out. Scanning the bus routes, I headed for the Burn Center in New York Hospital to see Terry Campbell. Of the 11 firefighters who were burned, Terry was the most serious case. All the others were treated and granted medical leave; three of them were admitted to Coney Island Hospital in Brooklyn.

I didn't bother to call first to check visiting hours, because I thought surely they would not deny me a visit as a fellow fire-fighter. But if they did, at least I would find out about the visiting hours firsthand.

I met Terry in 1975, shortly after transferring into Ladder 153. Like myself, he also worked in Ladder 102 but had transferred out before I was assigned there. He had told me how much he liked working in 153 because "it wasn't too busy or too slow, but just right!" And there was "enough work [fire duty] to keep your skills intact."

Although I arrived at the Burn Center before visiting hours, I was allowed to see him. However, the staff asked me not to stay too long and also to tell everyone else to please come during visiting hours only.

XXXXXXXXXXXXXXXXXXXXXXXXXXXXXXXXXXXXXXXXXXXXXXXXXXXXXXXXXXXXXX

They were very nice, but also emphatic about the visiting rules because, among other reasons, they knew he would be getting a lot of visitors.

They made me wear a cap, gown and face mask. Actually seeing him was somewhat of a shock. His head was very pink and swollen due to the body fluids that accumulate in the area of a burn, and his hair and eyebrows were gone. Obviously, his helmet flew off as he went down with the burning roof. All he remembered, except thinking that he was going to die, was Firefighter Harry Latting of Engine 254 pulling him out.

I didn't bring it up, but somehow he already knew about George and Jim. We spoke for a while, and I was glad my face was covered by the mask. Only my eyes were exposed and I hoped he didn't notice that they were getting moist. As promised, I didn't stay too long.

While removing the cap, gown and mask by the laundry bin, I became aware of one good reason why they didn't want visitors at other than designated times. Part of the treatment for burn patients is "debridement," which is the removal of dead skin in order to help the healing process and prevent infection.

XXXXXXXXXXXXXXXXXXXXXXXXXXXXXXXXXXXXXXXXXXXXXXXXXXXXXXXXXXXXXX

XXX

Unfortunately, it is very painful. Before leaving, I would hear the screams of a boy having his skin pulled off.

I was scheduled to work that night, so I headed back to Brooklyn. At the firehouse, I spread the word about the strict visiting hours, but not about the screaming boy.

While Terry's condition improved, the doctors advised him to take plenty of fluids. When he was told it was OK to drink beer, naturally we complied; with discretion, of course, using styrofoam coffee cups.

Very often, at the sight of a styrofoam cup, I would recall how much he enjoyed the beer we brought him. A simple pleasure, that but for the grace of God he might never have experienced again.

As a result of his disabling injuries, Terry was eventually retired from the Fire Department.

*   *   *

XXXXXXXXXXXXXXXXXXXXXXXXXXXXXXXXXXXXXXXXXXXXXXXXXXXXXXXXXXXXXXXXXXX

THE FUNERALS

August 4, 1978: This morning, Daniel Stromer, Brooklyn Trustee of the Uniformed Firefighters Association (UFA) came to the firehouse. He said the City offered to pay all funeral costs if the families agreed to one mass ceremony; they did not. All six funerals were held separately; two on Saturday, the 5th, and four on Monday, the 7th.

The wakes, of course, were held separately. I would describe them, but I must confess that I did not attend any of them, except for Jim McManus' on the morning of his funeral.

There is something about wakes that is very unnerving, and I am especially uncomfortable about attending them, so I usually do not. Even the term "wake" presupposes a curious origin.

FUNERAL DAY I

August 5, 1978: Although the funeral Mass for Jim McManus was to be at St. Adalbert's Church on Staten Island, his body was laid out in a funeral parlor within walking distance (about 1/2 mile) of my apartment in Brooklyn.

It was a cloudy morning with an ever-threatening rain. I had brought my dress uniform home, but not the raincoat. Unless there is a downpour, nobody likes to wear the raincoat anyway, because it is an unflattering swatch of wrinkly dark blue vinyl, and it conceals all decorative insignia that are proudly displayed above the left breast of the uniform jacket.

The service ribbons represent medals, unit citations or other meritorious awards. There is a regulation prohibiting the display of more than five such insignia, but I've often seen members with at least twice that number. To my knowledge, that rule has never been enforced.

Inside the funeral parlor, next to the closed casket, was an 8x10 photo of Jim taken when he turned 1st grade, more than 14 years before. Looking noticeably younger in the photo, perhaps he would have aged differently had he chosen a different vocation.

After saying a prayer for him, I recognized a former member of Ladder 153 from his visits to the firehouse. He was now a Fire Marshal. I remember him looking at the casket and the photo. Suddenly, he broke down in grief and had to excuse himself.

xxxxxxxxxxxxxxxxxxxxxxxxxxxxxxxxxxxxxxxxxxxxxxxxxxxxxxxxxxxxxxx

Just before taking the casket from the funeral parlor is a time that the immediate family should have some privacy. I went outside and stood by with some other members until Jim was placed in the hearse and driven away to the church.

Catching a ride with some guys, we went over the Verrazano Bridge to Staten Island. While looking for a place to park, we saw hundreds of uniforms gathering to fall into formation along the street in front of St. Adalbert's church.

After the ceremonial officers lined everyone up (about two thousand now), the casket was driven to the church atop a fire engine with several firefighters marching along each side and to the rear.

It was raining now; but a soft, gentle rain.

During the time the casket is removed from the pumper and carried into the church, and upon proper commands, all uniformed personnel stand at attention while saluting. After the deceased member and his family are inside, city officials and other VIPs enter and then everyone else. Mayor Koch was there, bless his heart, in a gray suit that looked like he had slept in it.

I've never seen a line-of-duty funeral, including this one, at which the church could accommodate all present. Usually, each end of the formation is so far away, you can't see or hear anything. As members of Jim's firehouse (L.153 and E.254), we were designated a place in the formation to assure entry into the church.

Inside, next to me, sat Firefighter Joe Sheehan of Engine 254. He always reminded me of the famous comedian W.C. Fields with his sharp wit and humor, but during the Mass, this jovial, funny man was muffling a sob. To this day, I don't know why I didn't put my arm around him. Maybe because he was older than me, maybe I didn't want to draw any attention, or maybe I'm just a big dope, I just don't know. Joe passed away not too long after he retired a few years ago.

After the Mass, everybody lined up again, and the casket was replaced on the pumper. As a final farewell, the hand salute is held until the deceased passes the end of the formation.

This same ritual was performed this morning at St. Luke's Church in Brentwood, New York, for Lieutenant James Cutillo. The remaining four funerals were scheduled for Monday.

XXXXXXXXXXXXXXXXXXXXXXXXXXXXXXXXXXXXXXXXXXXXXXXXXXXXXXXXXXXXXXXXXX

After the customary collation, I caught a ride back to Bay Ridge with some members who had to report back to their units. As they were officially detailed to the funeral, they had a Department car. Via the radio, we heard a 2nd alarm fire in progress; a vacant building in Sheepshead Bay. Luckily, it was uneventful. I was dropped off on 3rd Avenue, where I was about to break another regulation by entering a tavern while in uniform.

I suppose it's normal for a bar in a working class neighborhood to be fairly busy on a Saturday afternoon with the local regulars, and Feeley's was no exception. As I entered, some fellow made a somewhat mocking gesture by raising his hands in the air and saying, "I didn't do it!" Obviously, he was "under the influence" and might have thought I was a police officer. Perhaps he was attempting to show off in front of his friends, or more than likely, he was just a jerk.

I ignored him and went toward the other end of the bar to find a belly-up space. The bartender was busy, so I had to wait a couple of minutes to be served. Meanwhile, I noticed all the patrons drinking and engaged in their conversations. I finally got served and keeping to myself, proceeded to sip my drink.

XXXXXXXXXXXXXXXXXXXXXXXXXXXXXXXXXXXXXXXXXXXXXXXXXXXXXXXXXXXXXXXXXXX

Adding to all the noise of talking was a radio on a shelf behind the bar. It wasn't long before a news report of the two funerals that day was broadcast. I was the only one who heard it because, as I looked around the bar not one person, not even the bartender, paid attention to it, or me. Again I felt angry, because no one there had the social consciousness to link my uniform with the current events in his city.

Thinking back, those people were not there to listen to the news. They were unwinding from a week at the office, or staying away from a nagging spouse, or had nowhere else to go and no one to go with, or whatever.

In the Billy Joel song, "Piano Man," he says people came to see him "to forget about life for a while." But how does a firefighter forget about life when he is perpetually prepared to save it?

How does he forget about life after seeing so much death?

I finished my drink and went home.

*   *   *

FUNERAL DAY II

August 7, 1978: I was scheduled to work today, but in the fire service, unlike most jobs, you can't just call in to take a day off, even if it is to attend a funeral. Nor can we place a sign in front of the firehouse that says, "Closed Due to Death in Family."

The solution is to allow off-duty members of other units to volunteer to work for those attending the funerals. I was to be the chauffeur that day, so I needed a replacement who was trained to drive and operate a *tower ladder.

Before today, Firefighter Charlie Larson of Ladder 172 made himself available to work for anybody in the firehouse. A qualified chauffeur, he took my place. I had worked with Charlie in 172 for about two years. He seemed to have a great outlook on life and got along with everybody. And everything he did had to be done just right. A bit meticulous, yeah, that's the word!

*A fire truck that almost all reporters incorrectly call
a "cherry picker."

XXXXXXXXXXXXXXXXXXXXXXXXXXXXXXXXXXXXXXXXXXXXXXXXXXXXXXXXXXXXXXXXX

xx

Charlie was also a motorcycle enthusiast and we rode together on several trips. One trip, which he organized, was a ride on the Garden State Parkway in New Jersey on the first day motorcycles were permitted. Until then, motorcycles were banned to "keep it safe," but some bikers took the ban to court and won. So Charlie thought it would be a good way to piss off the New Jersey authorities.

They had to allow us on the road but there were signs prohibiting use of the exact change lanes at the toll booths. Lest we mess up their traffic count at every toll, the collectors, with worried looks, would say, "One at a time, one at a time!"

Charlie rode solo a lot and some years later had a serious accident when a truck ran him off the road. He told me about it at a retirement party for Battalion Chief McQuade (Batt. 33). Although he recovered physically, he said he'd never ride again. I assume he figured he had covered enough miles and thought, "Why push my luck?"

It's hard to say how many members decided to retire from the Department as a direct result of the Waldbaums fire or any other serious fire. I happen to know of several, but it's not like they actually said, "I don't want to push my luck!"

xxxxxxxxxxxxxxxxxxxxxxxxxxxxxxxxxxxxxxxxxxxxxxxxxxxxxxxxxxxxxxxxxx

Some things you just know, right?

Some time after the fire, I was at the housewatch area of the firehouse with Firefighter Robert Dwyer of Engine 254. He was sitting at the watch desk and while looking down at the floor he said, "I gotta get out of this fuckin' job!" And he did, as soon as he could. Likewise, Firefighter Bennis, chauffeur of Ladder 153, who had taken the company to the fire, and placed some members on the roof via the bucket of the tower ladder.

After 20 years service, you needn't give a reason for retiring. Before that, you must be declared unfit by the Bureau of Health Services, no matter what reason you give.

Of the four funerals held today, I would attend that of my co-worker in Ladder 153, George Rice. My dress uniform still at home, I went directly to Resurrection Church. It was pretty far, but I only had to take two buses.

On the second bus, the air conditioning system wasn't working, so I opened a window. Then an old lady sat by the window and closed it. Here it is, a hot August morning in New York and I'm standing in a crowded bus wearing a wool uniform, and this

XXXXXXXXXXXXXXXXXXXXXXXXXXXXXXXXXXXXXXXXXXXXXXXXXXXXXXXXXXXXXXXX

XX

idiot closes the window like maybe she's going to catch pneumonia. Silently, I wished I hadn't sold my car and wondered why I didn't ride my motorcycle to the church.

Finally, the bus reached Gerritsen Avenue and I got out. As other members arrived and assembled in front of the church, a firefighter drove up in a Department car. Apparently, there was a snafu with the details, because they needed some members for an honor guard escort. In no time, seven or eight of us piled into a couple of cars and lined the steps in front of the funeral parlor.

The hearse was parked by the curb, its rear door open. A while later, George was carried out and down the steps between us as we saluted. After the hearse door was closed, we got back in the cars and met the fire engine (pumper) that was parked on Burnett Street, two blocks from the church and out of sight of the assembling formation.

Waiting with the fire engine were some members who the day before, were trained in, and practiced how to be pallbearers. Only they were allowed to place the casket on and remove it from the pumper. After the hearse arrived, this task was completed and we were ready to proceed to the church.

XXXXXXXXXXXXXXXXXXXXXXXXXXXXXXXXXXXXXXXXXXXXXXXXXXXXXXXXXXXX

One of the detailed pallbearers was Firefighter Dave Ireland, who I knew from Ladder 102, where he was still assigned. Dave was one of those guys with a body as solid as concrete and just as strong; a desirable trait in the fire service. Today he had to use that strength to fulfill a grievous, but necessary function.

Upon the order to proceed, the driver started the engine and drove to the church, using only the brake to control speed, as we walked along both sides of the pumper carrying George atop.

Everything went much the same as Saturday, except that I didn't see Mayor Koch, so I don't know if he had his gray suit pressed or wore a different one. Representing the Office of the Mayor was Herman Badillo, a handsome, well dressed gentleman who chose to project a different image than Koch. Regrettably, I cannot recall his official title at the time.

After the Mass, we again escorted the fire engine as it passed the formation. At a location away from the church, the hearse was waiting to receive the casket for the trip to the cemetery. Before the hearse door was closed, I put my hand on the casket and silently said, "Good bye, George!"

XXX

I'm sure there was a collation somewhere, but I chose to go to the firehouse and relieve Charlie. Even after I changed into my work uniform, he was still offering to stay and let me have the rest of the day off. I really appreciated what he did and thanked him, but there was nothing else I'd rather have done that day than finish my tour.

Well, that's the way I saw it, more than 13 years ago. Incredibly, I do not recall anything that happened the rest of that day, even though virtually everything on the preceding pages was from memory.

Some memories never fade away!

*   *   *   *   *   *

XXXXXXXXXXXXXXXXXXXXXXXXXXXXXXXXXXXXXXXXXXXXXXXXXXXXXXXXXXXXXXXXX

Unveiling and dedication of Waldbaum Fire Memorial Stone

Ladder 153 Firefighters Jack Tracy (l) and Vito Mattia

XXXXXXXXXXXXXXXXXXXXXXXXXXXXXXXXXXXXXXXXXXXXXXXXXXXXXXXXXXXXXXX

XXX

"For Firemen, Sadness is Part of the Job"
Pranay Gupte
New York Times, 8/4/78

PART 3

"A POEM AND TWO LETTERS"

Exactly one month after the fire, Lt. Ed Smith felt a need to write the poem, "Were He Not There," which turned out to be a tribute to all firefighters. It was his way of dealing with the tragedy and his feelings at the time.

Back then, terms such as crisis intervention or critical incident stress were unheard of, and professional counseling was not encouraged. I suppose it was assumed that we would automatically learn to accept death as part of the job.

XXXXXXXXXXXXXXXXXXXXXXXXXXXXXXXXXXXXXXXXXXXXXXXXXXXXXXXXXXXXXXXXXXXXX

As a probie, I recall how well the senior members reacted when there was a fatality. I learned to act tough by watching them, but now I know there must have been times when they were hurting inside.

Virtually all emergency rescue personnel can handle the inevitable casualty. It's the multiple deaths, uniformed or civilian, and small children that tear us apart.

Ed Smith later originated the Company Officer's Association in order to improve representation of captains and lieutenants, the Department's first line supervisors. He then went on to serve on the executive board of the Uniformed Fire Officers Association, Local 854, ultimately attaining the position of president. It is no exaggeration to state that he exemplifies compassion, nobility and brotherly love.

Following Ed's *poem is a letter from a British firefighter and then a letter from Carole Ann Rice. Both are self-explanatory.

*"Were He Not There," (c) 1978 by EJS.

XXXXXXXXXXXXXXXXXXXXXXXXXXXXXXXXXXXXXXXXXXXXXXXXXXXXXXXXXXXX

Were He Not There

Were he not there
The bold and brave
The man who took the oath to save
both life and property from fires harm
Who answers swiftly each alarm

Were he not there
This valiant son
His calling the most dangerous one
Who knows that once the oath he gave
May someday take him to his grave

Were he not there
Both day and night
To challenge fires endless plight
Then many more would feel the pain
Inflicted by the fires reign

Were he not there
This man so brave
His hopes and dreams he risks to save
Your life and property from fires harm
Dear God! Go with him to each alarm

And keep him always in thought and prayer
For perish the thought;

Were he not there

Inspired By The Memory Of
Six Firefighters Who Made The
Supreme Sacrifice at Brooklyn
Box 44-3300 On Aug. 2, 1978

Lieut. Ed Smith
Lad. Co. 153, 33rd Batt.
12th Div. N.Y.F.D.
9-2-78

*As a British fireman, may I offer our
Service's sympathy to you, and others
concerned, at the loss of your firemen's
lives on August 2, 1978.
        Although we may be 3000 miles apart, we
feel the same pain in these circumstances.*

P.A. Clark
Burton-on-Trent, England

(One of many letters and telegrams to FDNY from all over the world)

Source: WNYF, 3rd issue of 1978.

xxxxxxxxxxxxxxxxxxxxxxxxxxxxxxxxxxxxxxxxxxxxxxxxxxxxxxxxxxxxxxxxxxxxxxxx

XXX

To the Bravest Men I Know

I am writing to all of you at this time to express my feelings of pride and warmth you have given me and my children. The sense of compassion and respect has been overwhelming, and I'll never be able to put into words all of my feelings. I will always be proud to know that my husband George will be remembered as a member of a very special brotherhood of men. Even under the circumstances that took his life, I know you men will continue your jobs to the best of your ability to preserve life our most precious gift.

I'll never forget how people all over the United States wrote to me about the manner in which all of you brothers helped to ease what I feel to be four of the most difficult days of my life. The world not only looks upon me at this time but at all of the exceptionally brave men that constitute the N. Y. C. Fire Dept.

I ask God to help me and all the other wives that have lost their loved ones, and to protect all of you and give you strength now and always.

May God bless you all and keep you
in His care.

Mrs. Carole Ann Rice

XXXXXXXXXXXXXXXXXXXXXXXXXXXXXXXXXXXXXXXXXXXXXXXXXXXXXXXXXXXXXXX

DAILY◉NEWS
NEW YORK'S PICTURE NEWSPAPER®

220 E. 42 St. (212) 949-1234

Published every day by New York News Inc., 220 East 42d St., New York, N.Y. 10017. W. H. James, President and Publisher; Michael J. O'Neill, Editor and Vice President; Joseph F. Barletta, Vice President and General Manager; and R. C. Schneider, Secretary-Treasurer.

Mail subscription rates per year: U.S. Daily and Sunday $135.00. Daily $90.00. Sunday $45.00. Armed Forces Special Rates: Daily and Sunday $90.00. Daily $60.00. Sunday $30.00. Foreign and short term rates upon request.

Copyright New York News Inc. 1978. The Associated Press is entitled exclusively to the use for republication of all local news printed in this paper. All other rights reserved.

A SPECIAL BREED

It all happened with horrible suddenness.

One minute, firemen were working their way over a roof to fight the blaze. The next, they were plunging into the flames below.

Reflection of Tragedy

In that instant, six brave men died "in the line of duty."

Every firefighter — and every policeman, too — knows it can happen.

They may ignore the danger, bury the fear. But deep inside, they realize that there is no such thing as a "routine" fire or a "safe" patrol.

Most people could hardly imagine working under such conditions. Cops and firemen must do it, day in and day out. It takes a special kind of person, with a special kind of courage.

We lost six of those good men on Wednesday, in Brooklyn. Six men with wives and children, with hopes and plans. Six men who gave their lives in the name of duty, in service to their city.

Remember them. And remember, too, the thousands of other firemen and policemen whose ordinary duties so often demand an extraordinary valor.

From The New York Daily News, August 4, 1978.

XXXXXXXXXXXXXXXXXXXXXXXXXXXXXXXXXXXXXXXXXXXXXXXXXXXXXXXXXXXXXXXXXX

"We cannot understand firemen; they have risen to some place among the inexplicable beauties of life."

Murray Kempton
New York Post, 8/3/78

PART 4

"NEWSPAPER COVERAGE"

As I mentioned in the Introduction, the newspapers did an excellent job covering the fire. In the following pages, you will see the actual news headlines, articles and photos.

Rather than have me take all this information and recount it, you can see for yourself how the journalists reported it, without my inevitable subjectivity.

Although the coverage was excellent, it wasn't perfect, but what is? Most errors were trivial or "typos" and not worth fussing over, but I felt that I should make the following corrections pertaining to the news item below:

Corrected times and wording as follows:

8:39   Alarm received by telephone call.

8:42   Engine 254 announced arrival at alarm box 3300.

8:45   Engine 254 transmits radio code 10-75 to assure full first alarm assignment of three engines and two ladders.

9:19   Division 12 orders "radio" mixer off.
       (This procedure allows only the dispatcher to hear the message.)

What the Tapes Say About the Fire

Here is the sequence of events at Wednesday morning's supermarket fire at 2892 Ocean Ave., Brooklyn, where six firemen were killed.

8:42—Alarm received by telephone call.

8:45—Engine Co. 254 reports a "working fire." Dispatcher sends three engines and two ladders.

8:49—"All hands" fire announced. Three engines and two ladders working.

8:54—Battalion 33 requests extra engine and ladder..

9:02—Second alarm sounded. Two engines and one ladder sent.

9:07—Engine Co. 245 instructed to stretch a line to the roof of the building.

9:10—Division 12 requests additional ladder and engine.

9:16—Division 12 again requests additional ladder and engine. Communications "difficulty" reported.

9:16—John T. Stancarone, assistant Brooklyn borough commander, reports he is responding to fire.

9:17—Third alarm requested by Division 12. Collapse reported by division aide on radio, with doctor and ambulance asked to respond. One ladder sent to fill third alarm.

9:18—Fourth alarm requested by Division 12. Three engines and two ladders sent.

9:19—Division 12 orders water mixer turned off. Dispatcher notified of collapse, with possible victims. Chaplain notified.

9:24—Daniel A. Kane, acting chief of the department, responds to call for extra rescue units and races to scene.

9:40—Emergency Medical Service sends additional ambulances.

9:49—Additional trucks requested by Brooklyn command.

10:52—Department sounds "Code 10-45," report of dead —six times.

From The New York Daily News, 8/4/78.

FINAL ★★★

DAILY ◎ NEWS

Showers likely today and tomorrow. Near 80. Details page 103.

Vol. 60. No. 34   New York, Thursday, August 3, 1978   Price: 20 cents

6 FIREMEN DIE AS ROOF FALLS

36 Injured in Brooklyn Blaze

Seconds Before Collapse

Moments before roof collapsed killing six, firefighters work atop Waldbaum's supermarket at 2892 Ocean Ave., Brooklyn. Collapse injured 36 others in worst single fire disaster in city since 1966.

Stories pp. 3 & 21; other pics centerfold.

FIRE: A War That Never Ends

XXXXXXXXXXXXXXXXXXXXXXXXXXXXXXXXXXXXXXXXXXXXXXXXXXXXXXXXXXXXXXXXXXXX

NEW YORK POST, WEDNESDAY, AUGUST. 2, 1978

The day the roof fell in...

Post Photo by Vic DeLucia, 8/2/78 (c) New York Post

XXXXXXXXXXXXXXXXXXXXXXXXXXXXXXXXXXXXXXXXXXXXXXXXXXXXXXXXXXXXXXXXXXXX

XXX

NEW YORK POST, WEDNESDAY, AUGUST 2 1978

...and six firemen died

Post Photo by Vic DeLucia, 8/2/78. (c) New York Post

XXXXXXXXXXXXXXXXXXXXXXXXXXXXXXXXXXXXXXXXXXXXXXXXXXXXXXXXXXXXX

DAILY NEWS, THURSDAY, AUGUST 3, 1978

Roof Collapse Sends Six Firemen to Death in Sea of Flames

Waldbaum's supermarket is boiling inferno after roof collapse that sent six firefighters plunging to their deaths.

News photo by Henry Kurland

News photo by Henry Kurland, 8/2/78.
"(c) New York Daily News, used with permission"

Opposite page:
Post photo by Vic DeLucia, 8/2/78. (c) New York Post.

XXXXXXXXXXXXXXXXXXXXXXXXXXXXXXXXXXXXXXXXXXXXXXXXXXXXXXXXXXXXXXXXXXXXX

TODAY
Chance of showers, 70s

TONIGHT
Chance of showers, 60s

TOMORROW
Chance of showers, 70s
Details, page 2

TV: Page 28

NEW YORK POST

WEDNESDAY, AUGUST 2, 1978 25 CENTS © 1978 The New York Post Corporation   Vol. 177, No. 220

FINAL
3:00 P.M. PRICES

DAILY PAID
CIRCULATION FOR **609,822**
LAST 3 MONTHS

6 FIREMEN KILLED

Roof falls in Brooklyn store blaze

A fireman tries to console a comrade crying over the loss of their buddies in today's blaze that killed six.

Post Photo by Vic DeLucia

By Larry Nathanson
and Leo Standora

Six firemen were killed today when they plunged through the burning roof of a Brooklyn supermarket while battling a spectacular four-alarm blaze.

It was the worst disaster for the city's fire department in 12 years.

Twenty-six other firemen and one cop were injured — most of them in desperate efforts to dig through the burning rubble to find the firemen trapped inside.

Most of the injuries were minor, mostly smoke inhalation, but three firemen

More stories and pictures on Pages 2,3 and 13

were reported seriously burned and two others were undergoing examinations for possible heart attacks.

The names of the dead were not immediately released.

All of them had been trapped in the ruins of Waldbaum's at 2892 Ocean Av. at Avenue Y, in Sheepshead Bay.

Cranes and helicopters summoned to remove chunks of the store's roof that collapsed failed to arrive in time.

The one-story, half square-block brick and cin-

Continued on Page 13

FIRE: A War That Never Ends

From The New York Post, 8/2/78. Reprinted with permission:

Continued from page 1

der block building was virtually gutted.

Sanitation foreman Adolph Stampfel said he was in the neighborhood when the blaze erupted shortly before 9 a.m. and saw the burning building "swallow up" the firemen.

"There must have been 20 men on the roof cutting a hole open with flames coming up around them...then they just disappeared," said Stampfel.

"The roof caved in and I could hear them screaming and yelling. Some reached the edge of the roof (on the Avenue Y side) and hung there by their hands until other firemen got ladders to get them down. It was chaos. I don't know how many fell in but they just disappeared."

Vincent Wagner, a retiree who lives across the street, said the collapse occurred in a new wing being added to the store.

"They'd added a double roof because too much water had been collecting on it. They covered it with plywood and tar paper, and it looks like the fire got underneath it, and it exploded."

Wagner said he didn't think the firemen knew they were on a false roof.

Fire Commissioner Augustus Beekman, who took personal command of the rescue efforts, said the firemen would have been "pulled back" if there had been any indication that the roof was "unstable."

"But it happend too fast...withing warning...they fell right into the heart of the fire," Beekman said.

Beekman said the high injury toll occurred because "once we have men trapped, the other firemen will over exert trying to effect the rescues. You can't do that safely."

Rescue parties began clawing at the building when the fire was brought under control at 10 a.m. But by this time the six firemen had been trapped for nearly an hour.

Crews hastily formed from the more than 150 firefighters at the scene used a steel battering ram to smash a hole in a foot-thick wall on Avenue Y. Others used power saws to cut through steel beams to open a path for rescuers.

During the attempt to reach the trapped men rescuer after rescuer emerged from the building, gasping for air, their faces covered with soot, their eyes tearing. Some had to be dragged from the building themselves.

One fireman stumbled from the ruins of the building, slumped on the running board of a truck, then covered his face with his hands and began to weep. He was heard calling out the name Ed, a comrade who was apparently one of those trapped.

Mayor Koch, who rushed to the scene from City Hall, called the deaths a "tragedy that demonstrates the valor of men willing to lay down their lives for the public. It shows us how much we owe our cops and firemen."

Witnesses said that there were a number of customers in the store when the blaze broke out and many, believing there was no danger, continued to do their shopping.

"Nobody knew it was that bad," said a cashier. But she said everyone was quickly ordered out of the store and none of the customers or employes was injured.

The cashier added that "some people — would you believe it — wanted to be checked out" with their groceries.

All of the injured firemen were taken to Coney Island and Kings County Hospitals.

Terrence Campbell, 46, was transferred to New York Hospital-Cornell Medical Center's burn center with second degree burns over 12 per cent of his body.

At Coney Island Hospital, 40-year-old John Madigan of Ladder Co. 169, said he was on the roof when it caved in.

"We were hosing the roof with water, when it started to go," said Madigan who suffered cuts on his legs.

"It felt like I fell three stories. It was roasting. It was so hot you could light your cigarets in it. I was saying my prayers."

Nearby Jim Kowsky, 40, of Engine Co. 246, said he was alive because "I jog four miles a day and I've got good wind pressure."

Kowsky said he had 30 pounds of equipment on his back when he plunged through the roof, "but I made it to a side wall in six seconds through the fire and smoke. I told myself 'you'd better do it or you'll get roasted here.'"

Just six days ago, 19 firemen had to be hospitalized after being overcome by noxious fumes from burning Christmas tree ornaments while battling a blaze in the cellar of John's Bargain Store at 526 E. 14th St. across the street from Stuyvesant Town.

Today's death toll was the largest the department has suffered since 12 firefighters died in a blaze that destroyed three buildings in Manhattan's Madison Square at Broadway and 23d St. on Oct. 17, 1966.

That was the worst disaster in the history of the department with 10 of the firefighters perishing under a collapsed ceiling and two from the heat of the fire.

The last fire in which multiple deaths of firemen occurred was Feb. 8, 1976, when three firemen died fighting a blaze in Queens. The deaths today raised the number of firemen killed in the line of duty this year to seven.

Investigators said today's blaze was not considered to be of "suspicious origin."

TODAY
Cloudy, near 80

TONIGHT
Cloudy, near 70

TOMORROW
Cloudy, near 80

Details, page 2

TV: Page 24

NEW YORK POST

METRO
TODAY'S RACING

DAILY PAID
CIRCULATION FOR
LAST 3 MONTHS
609,822

THURSDAY, AUGUST 3, 1978   25 CENTS   © 1978 The New York Post Corporation   Vol. 177, No. 221

'He was on the roof, he waved to us and we waved back — then the roof collapsed'

Fireman's widow tells of his last seconds

By SHARON CHURCHER

William O'Connor's wife Louise and their three youngsters watched him die. "He was on the roof and he waved to us and we waved back. Then the roof collapsed," she said last night. "I knew it was over right there."

She knew. Yet to persuade herself it really happened, she watched it again on television, huddling with the children, her eyes widening with horror, as the evening news reported the supermarket blaze that took her husband and five other firemen.

"Is that Dad?" asked Billy Jr., 5, blonde, blue-eyed and the image of his father — he even wants to be a fireman too — as the camera focused on a slightly-injured firefighter being removed from the rubble.

"Dad's dead, right?" murmured his little sisters, Lisa Ann, 4, and Jeanne Marie, 2. The 29-year-old rookie fireman joined Ladder Co. 156 in Brooklyn only last December.

Previously, he was a transit cop, earning maybe a dozen citations, and before he served four years — including a tour in Vietnam — as a volunteer with the Navy.

"Ever since he was a child, all he wanted to be was a fireman. It's in the family," said his father, Harry, who is a captain with Ladder Company 168 and whose father was a fireman before him. "He took the Fire Dept. test when he was in the service but there was a freeze on hiring at the time."

The lanky young O'Connor married Louise, his childhood sweetheart, when he left the Navy and they set up house in an apartment at 70 Prospect Park Southwest, where he quickly established a reputation with neighbors as a one-man "rescue service".

"He was the first to help anybody out," said Bertha Kelly, the elderly tenant of an adjoining apartment.

Yesterday, O'Connor was due off-duty at 9 a.m. — but at a quarter of nine the all-hands alarm sounded.

Louise and the kids were at the firehouse minutes after, expecting to meet him and drive out to Breezy Point for a day with his sister.

"They (men at the firehouse) said, 'If the kids want to see a fire, go out to Ocean Avenue,'" she said, her face pale with grief.

As she talked, a phone call came through from the Fire Dept., inquiring whether her husband was wearing his official belt buckle when he left to fight his last blaze.

"You mean, they couldn't recognize him when they found him?" she begged his father. "You mean he looked so bad, they couldn't identify him without his buckle? Our three babies.....I can't believe it. He saw us, he was on the roof. Can you believe he's dead?"

...and six brave firemen plunged to their deaths

Tale of two wives: one who lost her man — one who found hers

By LARRY NATHANSON

The two women met, drawn by a bond, wives of firemen at a fire at which firemen died, each praying, "let it not be mine."

They climbed tangles of fire hoses, through puddles and debris passed crowds of cops and firemen and civilians.

Their eyes sought out the familiar face that would tell them there would be another time. For one there would be.

Helene Kenney, 41, got the word about 9:30 a.m. while at work as a receptionist for a physician. Her son called to ask if she knew about the big fire, not too far from their Brooklyn home. "Is Dad working?" he asked.

Mrs. Kenney has been married for 22 years to Bernard Kenney, a fireman for 20 of those years and a cop for five years before that. "He always wanted to be a fireman," she said.

Mrs. Kenney dialed Ladder Co. 159. The firemen on duty said the company had rolled. There was no word. A radio broadcast said there might be firemen trapped. Again she called the firehouse. Still no word. The knot in her chest grew tighter.

"You better go," said her employer, Dr. Harold Zarowitz, whose office on Beverly Road is about 10 minutes from the fire.

As Mrs. Kenney reached the outer fringes of firefighters she called out: "My husband is with Ladder 159, have you seen him, Bernie Kenney?" No one knew. It had been an hour since she had got that call.

Carolyn Rice had a longer wait. A friend had driven her from Islip Terrace, L.I., more than an hour's drive normally. It was 1:15 p.m. when she got to the scene — five hours after the fire began. It was still burning.

Mrs. Rice, a pale woman in her thirties, her brown hair piled in a bun, wearing a white blouse and blue jeans, approached the area, her reddened eyes searching each face. Her lips trembled and a woman friend held an arm around Mrs. Rice's shoulder.

When Mrs. Kenney reached the scene, she quickly spotted her husband in the bucket of his ladder, helping direct a stream of water onto the burning ruins.

Feeling the tension leave her in a tremendous sigh of relief, she headed towards the cluster of waiting ambulances.

She had been there some time when she saw Mrs. Rice and recognized the familiar desperate look in her face. "I understand what you feel. My husband is here too."

Mrs. Kenney put her arms around the younger woman and they walked towards the front of the supermarket. Mrs. Rice called up to a fireman on a ladder. It was Bernard Kenney. "My husband is George Rice, with Ladder 156, is he okay?"

Kenney pointed towards several fire officials. Mrs. Rice picked out a short black man with the white hat of a fire official. It was Commissioner Augustus Beekman, former chief of the department and a former fireman. She told him her husband's name.

"I could see in his eyes he didn't like the job he had to do," said Mrs. Kenney. "He's a good man."

Beekman checked with an aide who had a clipboard. He spoke with Mrs. Rice.

George Rice, 38, himself a fireman's son, had died with five others.

"Oh God no," Mrs. Rice screamed. Her legs sagged and Mrs. Kenney led her to the back of an ambulance.

"Georgie, don't leave me," she sobbed. They gave her smelling salts and comfort. Then, impelled by a small hope, Mrs. Rice tried to run back to the scene.

"No, you made a mistake," she screamed. "God, please tell me it's a mistake." They had to strip her of her last hope.

Mrs. Kenney led the weeping woman past the fire trucks and grime-smeared firemen, along Avenue Y toward her friend's car. One off-duty fireman said as she left that when firemen see a grieving widow leave a fatal blaze it is like viewing a scene from their own graves.

"My boy won't be able to live without him," Mrs. Rice said as they walked. She had two children, adopted, a girl of eight and a younger boy.

"They are good men," Mrs. Kenney said of firemen. "There is something that separates them from other men."

She has two sons, James, 21 and John 19. Both have taken the test for firemen.

News photo by Ed Molinari, 8/2/78.
"(c) New York Daily News, used with permission"

XXXXXXXXXXXXXXXXXXXXXXXXXXXXXXXXXXXXXXXXXXXXXXXXXXXXXXXXXXXXXXXXX

XXX

From the New York Post, (8/3/78). Reprinted with permission:

NEW YORK POST

RUPERT MURDOCH   Publisher and Editor-in-Chief
ROGER WOOD   Executive Editor
JAMES A. WECHSLER   Editorial Page Editor
PETER MICHELMORE   Metropolitan Editor

Tragic questions

The tragic deaths of six firemen at a four-alarm blaze in Brooklyn yesterday raise profound questions about the state of fire protection in the city.

Preliminary investigation has found that not enough firemen arrived in time to break open the roof before it finally collapsed and trapped the victims. A change of shifts and lack of available manpower because of fiscal cuts that in four years have reduced the department's personnel by 2000 may, according to the firemen's union, have contributed to the sluggish response to the fire.

Equally puzzling is the issue of why the Fire Dept. was apparently not informed that an unstable "double roof" existed over the one-story structure, thereby making it unsafe to walk on. Finally, there is the troubling question of why cranes and helicopters summoned to remove the rubble of the building's rooftop did not arrive on time.

While nothing can return the lives of the fallen men, the city can best honor their memories by making certain that these questions are answered clearly and quickly.

Hollow space

RAIN ROOF (made of tar paper and plywood – bolted together without struts or supports normally used.)

NORMAL ROOF

Door

Hole made by firemen trying to reach trapped colleagues.

Building at 2892 Ocean Av.

Post diagram by John Langton

B'klyn Blaze Kills 6 Firemen

By VINCENT LEE, THOMAS RAFTERY, ALBERT DAVILA and DONALD SINGLETON

Firemen carrying injured comrade from Brooklyn supermarket yesterday.

News photo by Al Ott

Six firemen were killed and 36 persons—34 of them firemen—were injured yesterday morning when the roof of a burning Brooklyn supermarket collapsed, plunging a dozen firefighters into a sea of flames.

It was the worst single disaster for the New York City Fire Department since the Madison Square fire of Oct. 17-18, 1966, when 12 firefighters were killed.

The dead were identified as: Fireman George Rice, 38; Probationary Fireman William O'Connor, 29; Fireman James McManus, 48; Fireman Harold Hastings, 40; Fireman Charles Bouton, 38, and Lt. James Cutillo, 39.

Critically injured firemen were identified as Richard Smicuska, 25, and George Costanzo, 49.

The fire started at 8:40 a.m. on the mezzanine of Waldbaum's supermarket at 2892 Ocean Ave. in the Sheepshead Bay section of Brooklyn. Nearly 25 plumbers, electricians and other craftsmen were working on a major renovation of the store, and there were a half-dozen market employes and perhaps 15 customers in the building at the time.

By the time the first firemen arrived minutes later the building had been evacuated. Fire officials declared an all-hands alarm at 8:49 a.m. and made it two alarms at 9:02.

One of the last persons out of the store was Dominick Mezzapesa, a sheet metal mechanic employed by the Tri-State Sheet Metal Co. in Farmingdale, L.I. "I was up in the attic section, just under the roof, when I heard a female voice on the public address system say 'Get out of the store! It's on fire!'" Mezzapesa said.

Then, shortly after 9:15, with nearly 20 firefighters on the roof of the building, there was a loud cracking sound and the central portion of the roof fell in, sending up a gusher of flames and smoke. Screams were heard from the firemen falling into the center of the blazing supermarket.

Gloria Anglero, proprietor of the Pride'n'Groom Pet Store at 2010 Avenue Y, was on her way to work. "There were about 15 firemen on the roof," she recalled later. "There was a loud boom. It sounded like lightning. Some of the firemen were able to race to the sides of the roof. The rest fell, yelling and screaming, into the burning building. All those men, yelling and falling. God, all I could think of was their wives and children."

At 9.18, fire officials declared a third alarm, and then a fourth. Mayor Koch and Fire Commissioner Augustus Beekman were notified and both rushed to the scene.

The fire raged out of control until 12:29 p.m., but even while it was burning, firefighters chopped four holes in the concrete-block walls to pull the dead and injured out of the huge smoke-filled building.

The Emergency Medical Service took 36 victims to Maimonides, Coney

(Continued on page 21, col. 1)

From The New York Daily News, 8/3/78.
News photo by Al Ott, 8/2/78.
"(c) New York Daily News, used with permission."

XXXXXXXXXXXXXXXXXXXXXXXXXXXXXXXXXXXXXXXXXXXXXXXXXXXXXXXXXXXXXXXX

(Continued from page 3)

Island, Kings County and Long Island Jewish hospitals; 26 men were admitted for treatment. Of the injured, 34 were firemen, one was an Emergency Service police officer and one was an emergency medical technician. One fireman, Terrence Campbell, 46, was taken to the New York Hospital Cornell Medical Center Burn Unit. where he was admitted in "noncritical" condition with burns over 40% of his body.

Ironically, one of the improvements being installed in the supermarket renovation was a sprinkler system, which was largely in place but not in working order.

Various workmen said the fire broke out in a small aisle between a men's room and a compressor room on the mezzanine level of the market, which was being nearly doubled in area by the construction of an addition.

"I was working there on the mezzanine when I saw flames coming from a large wooden beam right next to the men's room wall," said Arthur Stanley, a plumber employed by the Bellkey Maintenance Corp. of Brooklyn, a subcontractor on the renovation job.

Hooked Up Garden Hose

"I told somebody to tell the store manager and then I hooked up this garden hose I keep in my tool kit, and tried to put it out. But it didn't do any good. Finally, we just had to run out."

Many of the workmen told reporters that the fire quickly spread into the compressor room, where there were compressors for more than 25 air conditioners and refrigeration units.

"I could hear popping sounds coming from the compressor room," said Cliff Marnick, an electrician.

Freon Gas and Oil

Joseph DeTemple who was rigging compressors when the fire broke out, said "the suction lines started to explode when it began to get hot, pouring freon gas and oil out."

Outside the market, the crowd grew as the first of an eventual 200 firemen and 38 pieces of apparatus arrived.

"There was a fire inside the building. I could see the smoke and flames," said Walter Capelli of 58 Bay 11th St. "There were firemen up on the roof. I heard a crash and the screaming. They never had a chance. I could hear them screaming and yelling as they fell. I ran over to help.

"We were all trying to pull them out," Capelli continued. "One fireman had a broken arm and was badly burned. I think we got four out. There was so much heat inside, it was so intense that we couldn't go very far."

One fireman who had been on the roof was Capt. Frank Gudelis of Engine Co. 243.

"I was at the front of the building," said Gudelis, soot-covered and lying on a stretcher in front of the building. "I was there when the whole thing fell out from under me. All I can remember is the sound, the roar of the roof collapsing, and then I didn't hear anything at all. I had my leg trapped momentarily, then the guys brought me out."

Batallion Chief Peter Eisemann was also on the roof. "I turned around to see if more units were arriving, and it happened," he said. "It just missed me — there but for the grace of God...."

The dead and injured were all out of the building even before the blaze was reported under control.

Several workmen said they had told firemen to use caution in walking on the roof. But fire officials said it was necessary for firefighters to be where they were when the collapse occurred.

"Standard Procedure"

"We recognize these kinds of fires as hazardous fires," said Fire Commissioner Beekman. "The roof collapsed with a degree of suddenness."

Koch confirmed that the deployment of men to the roof was "standard firefighting procedure," based on the judgment of superiors as to whether the roof is safe. "Sometimes that judgment is erroneous," Koch said.

"The trouble is there just isn't enough support with a roof like that — it's just like a big garage," said one fireman. "There's not enough beams, and sometimes the problem is complicated by heavy air conditioning units built into the roof. Roofs like that have killed firemen before."

Koch and Beekman were obviously moved deeply by the events of the morning.

"We have to appreciate the enormity of this tragedy," said Koch. "It goes to show how much we owe our dedicated police and firemen for the dangerous work they are willing to engage in."

"That's Our Job"

"It's very difficult for me to express my thoughts," said Beekman. "We are always sorry to lose men, but if there's another fire next door we just run to it. That's our job. After 113 years, (the age of the Fire Department) we know we will always be back. It's just our job."

"The toll of dead and injured firefighters goes beyond grief and shock to admiration for a department whose mortar is devotion to the community, and whose bricks are courage," said Gov. Carey in a statement.

"All New York is poorer because of the deaths of the six firefighters, but richer because we can say they were our protectors, as are all those who serve in fire and police departments," the governor concluded.

"These brave men jeopardized their lives—as they do every working day in an attempt to save the lives of others," said City Council President Carol Bellamy. "The loss is a great one...."

From The New York Daily News, 8/3/78.

XXXXXXXXXXXXXXXXXXXXXXXXXXXXXXXXXXXXXXXXXXXXXXXXXXXXXXXXXXXXXXXXXXX

Photo credit: William E. Sauro/NYT Pictures, 8/2/78.

XXXXXXXXXXXXXXXXXXXXXXXXXXXXXXXXXXXXXXXXXXXXXXXXXXXXXXXXXXXXXXXXXX

XX

Post photo by Vic DeLucia, 8/2/78. (c) New York Post

Chief Bishop (white fire helmet in foreground)
supervises handling of body bag.

XXXXXXXXXXXXXXXXXXXXXXXXXXXXXXXXXXXXXXXXXXXXXXXXXXXXXXXXXXXXXX

SIX FIREMEN KILLED AS ROOF COLLAPSES AT BROOKLYN BLAZE

TOLL IS WORST IN DOZEN YEARS

Burst of Flame Swallows Victims at Market — Union Charges Delay on Second Alarm

By JOHN KIFNER

Six firemen fell to their deaths as the blazing roof of a Brooklyn supermarket collapsed yesterday morning. It was the worst accident involving the city's firefighters in a dozen years.

As the roof suddenly erupted in a burst of flames, dropping men into the center of the fire, a handful of other firemen — members of the first ladder companies to reach the blaze — scrambled to the wall at the edge of the roof and held on until they were rescued.

"All of a sudden there was a terrible burst of flame," said Leonard Stone, a retired jeweler who lives across the street. "They all went down just like they were infants. It was a shame to see those fellows blown into the air, and then they just fell into the fire."

"There were a dozen guys up there, and they just disappeared into the flames," said Adolph Stampfel, an assistant foreman with the Sanitation Department.

Witnesses said it was then just about 9 A.M.

Koch Pays Tribute to Firemen

Tears streaking sooty cheeks, other firefighters pulled bodies of their comrades from the rubble and continued battling the flames at the Waldbaum's market in the Sheepshead Bay section.

Mayor Koch, grim-faced amid the tangle of hoses, water and thick smoke, said that "you realize the exceptional service people are willing to give to the city when they're willing to lay down their lives."

The Uniformed Firefighters Association, which is engaged in contract negotiations with the city and which has charged that cutbacks in manpower have endangered firemen, asserted that a lack of manpower and a delay in sounding the second alarm had contributed to the

150 Men Battle Flames

Some 150 firemen from 30 companies were called to the scene before the fire in the supermarket — which was undergoing renovation — was declared under control at 12:29 in the afternoon. Among the renovations was the installation of a sprinkler system — not yet working, according to Joseph A. Flynn, director of the Fire Department's support services unit.

The dead firefighters were identified as Firemen William O'Connor, Charles S. Boutan, George Rice, James T. McManus and Harold Hastings and Lieut. James E. Cutillo.

More than a score of other firemen

Continued on Page A16, Column 1

were taken to hospitals during the day. Most were released after treatment for smoke inhalation, but seven of the more seriously injured were admitted, including George Castanzo and Richard Smicuska, who were reported in critical condition last night at Coney Island Hospital.

In addition Fireman Terrence Campbell was reported in satisfactory condition at the burn center of the New York Hospital-Cornell University Medical Center after reportedly suffering second-degree burns over 12 percent of his body.

Twice, sobbing wives went to the supermarket at Avenue Y and Ocean Avenue where their firemen husbands had died.

"We do this every day of the week," Assistant Chief Daniel A. Kane was saying minutes after Fireman Rice's widow was led away by firemen. "This will happen."

The alarm for the fire was given at Brooklyn Box 44-3300 at 8:40 A.M. Within minutes, thick black smoke was billowing through the quiet, residential Sheepshead Bay neighborhood of brick apartment houses and single-family homes.

Inside the Waldbaum's store were some 30 contruction workers, about 10 supermarket employees and about as many customers. Virginia Moore, a cashier, said that a workman had cried that there was a fire in the men's room. She said she had picked up the microphone and warned people to get out of the store.

"Some people — would you believe it — wanted to be checked out," she recalled later.

The men from Ladder Companies 153 and 156 scrambled up to the roof, while those from Engine 254 began laying out their hoses.

The firefighters on the roof were seeking to "vent" the fire by chopping a hole. It was a standard maneuver, said the chief of department, Francis Carruthers, who rushed to the scene although he was

A battalion chief was on the roof, Chief Carruthers said, and had just reported over his radio that "'we're opening it up."

Suddenly the roof caved in.

Across Avenue Y, Walter Fullenwider watched the collapse from his Service Shoe Shop.

"It happened fast," he said. "It looked like hell to me. The flames were shooting very high, and the smoke was so thick in the street that you could hardly see. I heard a loud noise when the roof caved in and I saw five or six firemen running on the ledge.

"They looked like they were going to jump, and other firemen and people in the street started shouting, 'Don't jump, don't jump.' None of them jumped, and they got them down."

Firemen battered a hole in a brick wall to reach the charred bodies. Later, as hoses pumped water into the supermarket, a ladder and air tanks could be seen among the wreckage.

Fire Chaplain Alfred Thomas went into the burning supermarket and made the sign of the cross with oil on the foreheads of the six men, administering extreme unction, the emergency last rites of the Roman Catholic Church. As the bodies were taken out, they were covered with a white sheet or gray blanket, and the stretchers were place in ambulances.

Many of the firefighters cried. Some knelt in prayer.

Firemen O'Connor's wife and mother — his father is a fireman, too — went to the burning building. They had heard over television that firemen were trapped when the roof collapsed. Other firemen put their arms around the O'Connors and tenderly led them away.

By early afternoon, the department had set up an emergency center for the relatives at nearby Engine Company 321, where Deputy Commissioner Stephen J. Murphy held the grim news on six slips of white paper.

Mayor Koch, rushing to the scene, said the deaths were "hard to accept."

"It indicates," he said, "how much we owe our firemen. It's just overwhelming."

NY TIMES
8/3/78

Brief Biographies of the Six Killed in Blaze

Charles S. Boutan

Lieut. James E. Cutillo

Harold F. Hastings

James P. McManus

William O'Connor

George S. Rice

Several suitcases lined an otherwise empty hallway in the home of Harold F. Hastings last night, reminders of the vacation the family was planning to begin today at Walt Disney World in Orlando, Fla. Yesterday was to be Mr. Hastings' last day at work at the 156th Ladder Company before leaving with his wife and three children for their eagerly awaited holiday.

But Mr. Hastings and five other New York City firemen working with him plunged to their deaths yesterday when the flaming roof of a Brooklyn supermarket caved in.

Mr. Hastings, 39 years old, a fireman for 17 years and aide to the chief of the 42d Battalion, was remembered last night by relatives as a devout church-goer and a vital family man. The house in Hicksville, L.I., rang out with laughter Tuesday night as he built a house of cards with his children—Brian, 14; Christine, 12, and Dawn 10. He and his family were familiar faces at Holy Family Roman Catholic Church in Hicksville.

"He was simply a good man," said his sister-in-law, Mrs. Angela Sini. "And he was a fireman. It was his life, his everything."

•

JAMES P. McMANUS, a tall, husky fireman first-grade with a head of thick, curly white hair, was the man on his block in Graniteville, S.I., whom neighbors went to when they had a problem.

"He was always ready to help out," said one neighbor, "take people to the hospital, things like that."

Mr. McManus, who was 45 years old and had been a fireman more than 17 years, was also termed a devoted family man and an active worker in nearby St. Adalbert's Roman Catholic Church by friends. He had sent both his daughters, Caroline, 13, and Tara, 9, to Catholic schools, as his parents had sent him when he was growing up in the Bay Ridge section of Brooklyn.

•

GEORGE S. RICE, who, along with Mr. McManus, had been a member of Ladder Company 153, had also been energetically involved in his local Roman Catholic parish, St. Mary's, in Islip Terrace, L.I.

Mr. Rice, 38, who had been a fireman for 13 years was the son of a fireman and many of his friends and neighbors were policemen or firemen.

He was a tall man of medium build, "a very hard worker, always working a couple of jobs, with an enormous amount of energy," The Associated Press quoted Susan Ordway, a neighbor, as saying.

He is survived by his wife, Carol, and two children.

•

WILLIAM O'CONNOR, 29, whose father and grandfather were firemen, had been ending his tour of duty when the alarm for the supermarket fire rang, The Associated Press said.

"But he went anyway," the news agency quoted Pat Halprin, a friend of Mr. O'Connor since childhood, as having said.

"He always gave 1,000 percent to his work," Mr. Halprin said.

Mr. O'Connor was a probationary fireman who had been fighting fires only eight months, having graduated among the top of his class of recruits last December.

Tall and thin, with reddish-blond hair, Mr. O'Connor had lived with his wife, Louise, and three small children in the Prospect Park section of Brooklyn, where he had grown up.

•

CHARLES S. BOUTAN, also fit the mold of a family man, always involved in activities with his five children, the eldest of whom is 12. A fireman first-grade, he joined the Fire Department on Sept. 14, 1968. He had lived in Farmingville, L.I., for about 10 years and had developed into a hero of sorts to the neighborhood children.

He also was involved in the local Parent-Teachers Association with his wife, Catherine, and enjoyed camping and canoeing with his children.

•

JAMES E. CUTILLO, 39 years old, lived among more than a half-dozen firefighters in his neighborhood in Brentwood, L.I. Wives of some of those firemen joined his wife, Evelyn, in her home when she learned that her husband had been killed in the supermarket blaze.

Mr. Cutillo, a lieutenant and in charge of the roof party fighting the fire Wednesday, joined the Fire Department on April 6, 1963. He was remembered by neighbors as a tall, athletic Little League coach who "loved his wife, his kids and his job," as Edith Ward, a neighbor and wife of a fireman, put it. He had two children, Jimmy, 9 years old, and Gina, 12.

Re: pp. 80 and 81, "Copyright (c) 1978 by The New York Times Co. Reprinted by permission."

XXXXXXXXXXXXXXXXXXXXXXXXXXXXXXXXXXXXXXXXXXXXXXXXXXXXXXXXXXXXXXXXXXXXXXXXXXX

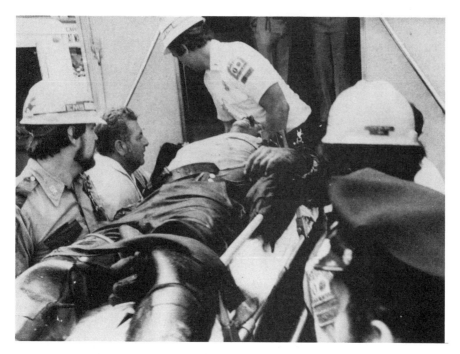

Above: Post photo by Hal Goldenberg, (c) New York Post, 8/2/78
Below: Photo courtesy of FDNY, 8/2/78.

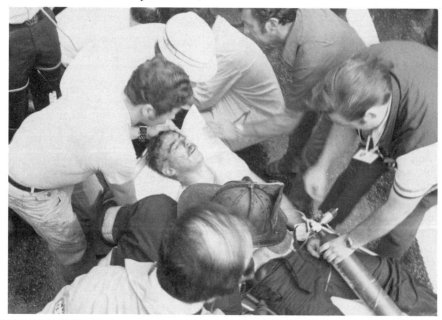

XXX

Post photo by Louis Liotta, (c) New York Post, 8/2/78

After treatment for burns at Coney Island Hospital,
Firefighter Hal Plaut and wife, Jane, listen to nurse.

XXXXXXXXXXXXXXXXXXXXXXXXXXXXXXXXXXXXXXXXXXXXXXXXXXXXXXXXXXXXXXX

Photo courtesy of FDNY, 8/2/78.

By early afternoon, most of roof and entire contents
of supermarket is reduced to smoldering debris.

XXXXXXXXXXXXXXXXXXXXXXXXXXXXXXXXXXXXXXXXXXXXXXXXXXXXXXXXXXXXXXXXXXXX

DAILY NEWS, THURSDAY, AUGUST 3, 1978   21

Brave Fire Women, Too Soon to Be Widows

By ALBERT DAVILA and DONALD SINGLETON

They came, frantic-eyed, while the flames and smoke still were pouring out of the rubble of the ruined supermarket. They drove up in well-worn station wagons and sedans, and they wore the rumpled clothes that women wear to do the housework, and they brought the kids with them; no time to get a baby-sitter.

They came, the wives of firemen, drawn by the bad news that always travels fast, drawn to learn which of them had just become firemen's widows.

A young, blonde woman with a blonde-haired baby in her arms steps over the hoses, walking fast, her eyes darting, searching faces.

Suddenly she spots a fireman, his face blackened by soot. He sees her at the same instant. They run toward each other and embrace, weeping in each other's arms. Those who see the couple come together find tears running down their faces.

"We used the radios to find them (the bodies)," said Fireman Anthony Matteo of Engine Co. 253 as he rested momentarily beside a fire truck. "We shut off all our walkie-talkies, and then they send a beeper signal out, and you could hear the beep from the guys' radios under the rubble."

They brought the bodies out one at a time, on stretchers. They put the stretchers in the ambulances and drove them off, and a lot of people stopped what they were doing and watched as the ambulances pulled away.

The off-duty firemen arrived in their day-off clothes. Quietly, they went to the trucks, slipped on boots and coats and hats and walked over to where the search for bodies was going on. The smoke still rose from what had been the roof of the building, and occasionally a brief orange tongue of flame

"What's going on, what's going on?" the man on crutches said, to no one in particular. "My brother-in-law, George Rice, works in Engine 153 and nobody will tell me what's going on. I'm down here trying to figure out what's going on and nobody will tell me if he's dead or alive."

A woman in her 30s, curly brown hair, blue eyes, runs away from a fire engine, where she has been talking to some firemen. She is Mrs. George Rice.

"Oh, God, no," she screams. "I want to go with him. I want to go with him. I love him, I love him. Oh, Georgie, don't leave me."

The emergency medical technicians put their arms around her and walk her into one of the big ambulances they call buses. She wilts like an unwatered plant, collapses in sobs.

One of the survivors was a fire sergeant, who lay on a stretcher, an oxygen mask covering his sooty face. Medical technicians said he had severe burns of the feet and one hand; he was twisting in pain. A fire captain bent near his face. "How ya doin', sarge?" the captain said. "Take it easy. Don't worry. Everything will be okay. I'm going to the hospital with you. You take it easy now." The sergeant nodded, gingerly. "He'll be okay," the medic said.

At 14, Son Is Now the Man of This Family

By RICHARD EDMONDS and GEORGE JAMES

"I have to take care of the family now because my father is gone," said 14-year-old Brian Hastings, speaking purposefully of his father, Harold, 40, who died a fireman's death. "He lost his dad, who was a mailman, when he was 14."

Hastings, a chief's aide, died with five others one day before he was to begin his vacation.

"He fixed up the whole car," said daughter Christine, 12, as they spoke in the bereaved quiet of the family's split-level home at 19 Petal Lane, Hicksville, L.I. "We were going to Disney World."

Lost Father, Then Husband

It was Fireman George Rice's first day back from vacation when he died. "When the news came, we all screamed," said Thomasina Caputo, 12, who like other neighborhood children in Islip Terrace, L.I., called Rice and his wife, Carol Ann, "Uncle and Aunt," and remembered that he played the organ for them. "Everyone on the block cried." Rice, 38, leaves two children, 4 and 8.

Fireman Charles Bouton's wife, Catherine, had lived the nightmare before. Bouton's brother-in-law, Terrence O'Reilly, said at the Bouton home at 20 Campus Drive, Farmingdale, L.I., "Catherine's father was also a fireman. Her father was killed when she was a little girl in New Jersey."

Catherine's mother is vice president of the Police and Firemen's Widows Association in New Jersey. Bouton leaves six children, 2 to 13. He gave up a job with the phone company to realize his dream of being a fireman, and did carpentry to make ends meet.

Fireman James McManus, 44, and his wife, Barbara, once talked of the dangers, said her closest friend, Florence Galligan, at the McManus' semi-attached, high ranch home at 145 Fieldstone Road, Staten Island. "She said she'd be afraid when he went on night. 'Why do you think it would happen at night?' he said. He was working days yesterday. Overtime."

Neighbors described McManus as a happy family man, a handy man, who always had time to help his neighbors with their swimming pools or take care of a cut on a neighborhood child's hand. "They're a very religious family," said Galligan. "She (McManus' wife) said to me maybe he was spared from something worse ... It was fate." McManus leaves two daughters, 9 and 13.

'He Was So Young'

Rookie fireman William O'Connor, 29, was to have spent the day picknicking and swimming with his wife, Louise, and their three children at Breezy Point.

People in their Windsor Terrace neighborhood in Brooklyn were "saddened," said a resident, Antoinette Sisto, who angrily said firemen and policemen should be paid what they want. "You tell me they're not worth what politicians are being paid?"

"This has been going around the neighborhood in people's minds," said Sisto. "There was no one in that fire to save. It's just a building. Let it burn ... It's so tragic because he was so young and it was a stupid way to go."

At the same time, at Lt. James Cutillo's home at 50 Thomas St., Brentwood L.I., Fire Lt. William Trica, a friend, was saying, "We are really out of one mold. We are taught to go into a fire. Not to stay outside. We may save a dog or a cat and that's all, but it's worth something to someone. ... They were doing their job."

Cutillo, a coach in the Brentwood Little League, had been a New York City policeman before joining the Fire Department. He leaves two children, 12 and 8.

Back in the Hastings' home in Hicksville, young Brian, who has some of his father's gear, said he and his dad saved a sleeping man's life in his burning house three years ago. "He was dedicated to the city," said one relative. "To the world," Brian interjected, perhaps speaking for all of them.

From The New York Daily News, 8/4/78.

XXXXXXXXXXXXXXXXXXXXXXXXXXXXXXXXXXXXXXXXXXXXXXXXXXXXXXXXXXXXXXXXX

Photo credit: William E. Sauro/NYT pictures, 8/2/78

Exhausted firemen reflect on their loss.

XXXXXXXXXXXXXXXXXXXXXXXXXXXXXXXXXXXXXXXXXXXXXXXXXXXXXXXXXXXXXXXXXX

XXX

Photo courtesy of FDNY

Fire Commissioner Beekman finally has time to
answer reporter's questions.

XXXXXXXXXXXXXXXXXXXXXXXXXXXXXXXXXXXXXXXXXXXXXXXXXXXXXXXXXXXXXXXXXXXXX

News photo by Jim Garrett, 8/3/78.
"(c) New York Daily News, used with permission"

Firefighters survey ruins the following morning.

XXXXXXXXXXXXXXXXXXXXXXXXXXXXXXXXXXXXXXXXXXXXXXXXXXXXXXXXXXXXXXXXXX

Top Officials and Union Debate Handling of Blaze Fatal to 6 Firefighters

By JOHN KIFNER

As the families and comrades of six dead firemen grieved and muncipal flags in New York City were lowered to half-staff yesterday, fire officials and the firefighters union debated the handling of the Brooklyn supermarket fire on Wednesday that turned into the worst fire tragedy here since 1966.

"It was almost classical," Chief of Department Francis Cruthers said, describing how the men from two ladder companies raced to the roof of the building to cut holes to "vent" the fire. "I thought the fire was fought well."

The Uniformed Firefighters Association, locked in contract negotiations with the city, renewed its charges that lack of manpower and a delay in sounding the second alarm in hopes of saving overtime costs had contributed to the tragedy.

"Death was the grim paymaster," said the union's president, Richard J. Vizzini.

The six firemen fell to their deaths when the roof of the Waldbaum's supermarket in the Sheepshead Bay neighborhood suddenly collapsed in a ball of flame, dropping them into the center of the blaze.

A Week of Mourning Ordered

Mayor Koch yesterday ordered all municipal flags lowered to half-staff and called for a week of mourning for the dead firemen. In the morning, in the quiet residential neighborhood, firemen on a tower ladder continued to hose down the smoldering supermarket at Ocean Avenue and Avenue Y.

The families of several of the men turned down a Fire Department offer of a single, group funeral at St. Patrick's Cathedral, such as the one that drew thousands of mourners to Fifth Avenue following the death of 12 firemen in an East 23d Street blaze in 1966.

The six firemen, however, will have the formal Chief's funerals that the department uses to honor those who have died in the line of duty, their wives agreed.

"Jim was very active in his church and I feel at home there," said Mrs. James McManus, explaining why she had selected St. Adalbert's Roman Catholic Church on Staten Island for her husband's funeral.

Against the background not only of the six deaths but of the ongoing contract negtiations — in which the manning of the fire trucks is an issue — Fire Department officials and union leaders debated the handling of the fire in back-to-back news conferences.

A fireman at Ladder Company 153 in Brooklyn reflects on the deaths of two of the company's men in Wednesday's fire

The union has long contended that the cutbacks in the number of firemen on each truck that were made during the city's fiscal crisis endanger the firemen and the public.

Mr. Vizzini said late yesterday that the Brooklyn District Attorney, Eugene Gold, had agreed to investigate the circumstances of the six deaths.

Only 22 men responded to the first call instead of the 30 that should make up a full complement, Mr. Vizzini contended, adding that under the standard practices three years ago, "a second alarm absolutely would have been sounded immediately."

"We charge that the city stalled on the second alarm for needed manpower in order to avoid paying overtime," he said, contending that the second alarm had been held back until after the day shift went on duty at 9 A.M.

"There was no delay in response," Fire Commissioner Augustus Beekman said in reply to the union's charges. "There was no consideration of overtime."

Standard Procedure Used

Asked about the union's contention that more immediate manpower could have averted the tragedy, Chief Cruthers said:

"I would say no. There's just as much chance more people might have perished."

Putting the men from the ladder companies on the roof to vent the fire — letting the heat and expanding gases escape — is the standard procedure in such fires, Chief Cruthers and other ranking fire officials said. But the roof had collapsed, and if more men had been on the roof, they, too, might have fallen through, the Chief indicated.

Mr. Vizzini did not question the technique of putting the men on the roof. "Roofs have to be vented," he said.

The roof of the Waldbaum's supermarket was a curved plywood structure, covered with tar paper and supported by wooden braces. There was a space of roughly four to six feet — known as a cockloft — between the roof and ceiling of the store.

Building Plans Called Proper

Such roofs are frequently troublesome, fire officials said, because they are subject to collapse if the braces are weakened and because the fire can "cook," or build up out of sight, in the cockloft.

Often, Commissioner Beekman said, investigations into such collapses show that they are caused by "some contruction quirk that obscures the recognizable signs that a roof is about to go."

Chief Cruthers said it appeared that the plans for the building were proper, but that investigators were checking to make sure they had been carried out according to specifications.

The fire, the officials and witnesses said, appeared to have begun in a small room, apparently housing air-conditioning equipment on a mezzanine, and spread into the cockloft, creating intense heat, but, at the start, little visible flame. A telephone call was received at 8:39 A.M., according to the department records, all first-alarm companies were called at 8:49; a call for more equipment was made at 8:55 and the second alarm sounded at 9:02.

Photo credit: Gary Settle/NYT Pictures

Copyright (c) 1978 by The New York Times Co.

Reprinted by permission.

XXXXXXXXXXXXXXXXXXXXXXXXXXXXXXXXXXXXXXXXXXXXXXXXXXXXXXXXXXXXXXXXXXXX

XXX

From The New York Post, 8/3/78. Reprinted with permission:

Probe will focus on 14 vital minutes and the double roof

Fourteen minutes may hold the key to the big question facing Fire Dept. investigators today. Why did six brave firemen plunge to their deaths in yesterday's Brooklyn fire tragedy?

The Uniformed Firefighters' Assn. charged last night that there had been an unnecessary delay in responding to the fire. The first alarm was sounded at 8.49 a.m. — but the second alarm, which would have rushed much-needed extra equipment to the scene, was not made until 9.03. Twelve minutes later, more than 30 firemen crashed into the flames when the roof collapsed over the blazing supermarket.

Fire Commissioner Augustus Beekman strongly denied the charges. And Mayor Koch insisted the Dept. had followed standard tactics.

But the Dept. is launching an indepth inquiry today. Among the other questions to be answered is: Were too many men sent up on the roof?

The architect who designed the building told The Post the roof was a curved rain-roof made of only tar and plywood. Asked if he would have stood on it, he said, "No."

$$s Not the Crunch at Fatal Fire: Survey

By VINCENT LEE and DONALD SINGLETON

No policy on the books of the New York City Fire Department would have caused any manpower shortage at the scene of last week's fatal Brooklyn supermarket blaze, a Daily News survey has shown.

The issue was raised on the day after the blaze by the Uniformed Firemen's Association president Richard Vizzini, who charged that penny-pinching city policies had led fire officials to delay putting in a second alarm moments before the building's roof collapsed, plunging six firefighters to their death.

"We conduct critiques on a borough-wide basis at which we outline these policies to all chiefs and company commanders," said Assistant Chief of Department Daniel Kane. "And the first thing we always stress is safety."

Overtime Considerations

Kane said commanders are monitored closely on their use of manpower, but added that the sword cuts both ways—"I've reprimanded chiefs when I've rolled in and they've had too little equipment," he said, "as well as when too much." he said.

Kane said the chiefs are told to give consideration to the clock only in the case of a fire in an abandoned and unoccupied building, where surrounding exposures are not occupied. "The chiefs are told to hold down overtime in cases like that if overtime would be involved," Kane said, "because there would be no worry about loss of life."

Fire Commissioner Augustus Beekman said the Waldbaum's Supermarket in Sheepshead Bay, Brooklyn, was considered "an occupied building—it was open and doing business, and in fact at the time of the announcement of fire, people were standing in line waiting to be checked out."

The Waldbaum's fire was reported at 8:40 a.m. on Wednesday. The firemen on duty had been working since 6 o'clock the previous evening, and would go on overtime status at 9 a.m. — in fact, many did.

(Firemen work a complicated schedule consisting of two nine-hour days followed by two days off, then two 15-hour days followed by three days off.)

Both Kane and Beekman stressed that commanders are instructed to spare no effort in the initial stages of a fire. "You can always send them back after they've got it contained," Kane said.

Edwin Jennings, president of the Uniformed Fire Officers Association, has differed with Vizzini, his fellow union leader, on the issue. Jennings said Friday that his members told him that overtime concerns and Fire Department manning policies played no part in the six firemen's deaths.

From The New York Daily News, 8/5/78.

XXXXXXXXXXXXXXXXXXXXXXXXXXXXXXXXXXXXXXXXXXXXXXXXXXXXXXXXXXXXXXXXXXX

TODAY
Showers, near 80

TONIGHT
Mostly cloudy, 60s

TOMORROW
Partly sunny, 80
Details, page 2

TV: Page 26

METRO
TODAY'S RACING

FRIDAY, AUGUST 4, 1978   25 CENTS   © 1978 The New York Post Corporation   Vol. 177, No. 222

DAILY PAID CIRCULATION FOR LAST 3 MONTHS   **609,822**

B'KLYN TRAGEDY: PROBE CLEARS FIRE DEPT.

Private investigators praise tactics

CRIMINAL charges are unlikely to result from Wednesday's supermarket fire that killed six firefighters.

An independent agency, which has launched its own investigation of the Sheepshead Bay tragedy, commended the Fire Dept.'s tactics as "good firefighting practice."

Bruce Teele, a fire service specialist at the Boston

headquarters of the National Fire Prevention Association, today was quoted as saying that "the action of opening up the building and ventilating it is accepted as good firefighting practice.

"I would say that they were following very accepted, good, standard firefighting practice."

The non-profit private association, founded in 1896, automatically sends investigators to examine any multiple-fatality fire to determine whether the fire fighting methods used conform to accepted protective engineering procedures.

David Demers, one of the agency's 200 staff investiga-

tors, arrived here yesterday to examine official reports on the fire.

His agency, which is devoted to working towards reducing fire fatalities, should conclude its investigation by next week, he said.

Meanwhile official law enforcement investigators here discounted the possibility of

criminal prosecution.

"Even if they (fire officials) did hold up the second alarm past 9 o'clock to save overtime," one source told The Post, "it is not a crime."

The preliminary findings of fire marshals, police and the Brooklyn District Attorney's office indicate that the four-alarm blaze at 2892 Ocean Av. was not deliber-

Continued on page 2

Continued from page 1
ately set.

Fire officials said there was "no indication of structural flaws" in the Waldbaum supermarket, which was undergoing renovation.

Demers, according to Teele, will try to determine whether there had been any alteration of the building "in which structural members were tampered with or perhaps weakened in some way so the building caved in quicker."

A spokeman for DA Eugene Gold said, "The entire mattter is under review to determine the truth about what happened."

She said an assistant DA

Truck driver's tribute

A long trailer-truck pulled up near the quarters of Ladder Co. 153 on Avenue U in Brooklyn yesterday. A young black man jumped out, fished dollar bills from his pocket and handed over $10 to firemen standing outside.

"When I realized that this was the firehouse where some of those men had died in the supermarket fire, it just came to me to try to do something to help the families...or toward flowers. I was in 'Nam, and I know the feeling when you see six men die horrible deaths." He said his name was Ronald Pettiford. He's 31 and lives in Jersey City.

was at the scene Wednesday while the fire was still raging.

Uniformed Firefighters Assn. President Richard Vizzini charged yesterday that the Fire Dept. had delayed sounding a second

alarm until after the start of the day tour at 9 a.m. "to save the overtime."

Fire Commissioner Augustus Beekman and Mayor Koch strongly denied the charge.

"There was no delay in

response," Beekman said. "There was no consideration of overtime."

The original alarm was sounded at 8:49 a.m. The second alarm came at 9:02. The roof collapsed at about 9:15, sending the firemen into the blaze. Third and fourth alarms were sounded at 9:17 and 9:19.

From The New York Post, 8/4/78. Reprinted with permission.

XXXXXXXXXXXXXXXXXXXXXXXXXXXXXXXXXXXXXXXXXXXXXXXXXXXXXXXXXXXXXXXXXXXX

Intense Heat Then a Chill in Heart

JIMMY BRESLIN

AUG, 3RD

The hats came off as the body was brought out through the hole they had chopped in the brick wall of the burning building. It is always the same: take off the fire-hat and hold it over the heart as the body of another fireman comes out.

A chaplain bent over the body, blessing it, as they carried it to an ambulance. The things that are often held in disdain suddenly are all you have.

"Who is it?" somebody said.

"Who knows, they're from 156 Truck and 153 Truck," a fireman said.

"The only one I know about is O'Connor. He's in 156 Truck. His wife showed up to pick him up after work this morning. By car. They live in Brooklyn. She had the two kids in the back seat. As she pulls up to the firehouse they leave. Leave for here. She follows them right to here. She got the kids in the back of the car and she follows them. She was here on the street someplace when it happened to him."

She was on the street watching when her husband went up the ladder and climbed onto the roof. William O'Connor waved to Louise and then turned and walked into the smoge on the roof. It collapsed and he tumbled to his death.

On the street, the women, hair messy from clutching at it, stand in the smoke and water puddles. These are the women the fashion magazines leave out and who are, on days such as yesterday, left to stand on Ocean Ave. in Brooklyn and look at a burning building and wonder if the husband inside the fire is alive or if he is one of the dead.

Three firemen were around one woman. "He isn't," she was saying, but there was no way to know what she meant.

"You're all right," one of the firemen said to her.

"He isn't!" she said again.

One of them held her and the others shifted their bodies to keep strangers away.

There are 18 children without fathers as a result of the fire in a supermarket on Ocean Ave. yesterday.

Tom Murphy stood on the side of

(Continued on page 71, col. 1)

(Continued from page 3)

the building, alongside the hole chopped in the wall, his eyes red and watery, his face a black mask, and he looked into the smoke out of which he had just crawled.

"Half our company was down below on the floor," he said, "and the other half was up in the crawl space under the roof. When the roof collapsed, four or five guys fell straight through to the floor. The other six guys got trapped in the crawl space. They didn't go all the way through to the floor and they got tangled up on the wire supports for the crawl space.

"Down on the floor, the one guy's face is all on fire. He's on fire here and here." Murphy was touching his arms and shoulders. "Fire all over him. You couldn't see the fire burning him, you could just see the fire all over him, you know? We got him out and all he said to us was, 'There's others in there in the third aisle. The third aisle of the supermarket.' That's all he said. He's got flames all over him and he tells us about others."

"Did you know who he was?" Murphy was asked.

"Tom Vellebouna, from Rescue 2," he said, "Jack Pritchard was with us. When he heard that, he went in and dragged one guy out and then he went back in and dragged two more out. He was something."

"Where's Pritchard now?"

"In the hospital."

From The New York Daily News, 8/3/78.

Across the street, John Madigan stood in a crowd with his wife. Madigan was still confused, but he was smiling. He had been on the roof when it collapsed. "There was no movement. It didn't shimmer or feel spongy or anything. It just collapsed. I wound up on a floor and I followed the light and came out. What light? God's light."

While Madigan spoke, three firemen stood on a cherry picker, well above the roof, and aimed their hose down at it. The fire smoke billowed as the water hit heat. One of the firemen was resting his chin on a hand as he watched the stream. Why, you wondered more didn't the day start this way, with firemen on equipment safely above the flames, instead of bunched on a roof whose support had burned away and soon would collapse under the weight of even a strolling cat?

Antiquated Firefighting?

And as you stood there and watched the men in the cherry picker safely throw water on the blaze, you wondered if New York's notions of firefighting, like its bookkeeping, could have gone out of date. Why, in an age of machinery, do 26 men have to stand on the roof of an empty building, with no lives at stake but their own, and use working methods that are at least a hundred years old?

"Fight a fire from the outside?" a lieutenant said. "That's the way the volunteer departments do it." He said that with disdain. He also had six dead.

The chaplains gathered in a firehouse on Gerritsen Ave. and looked at small slips with the names of the families of the dead written on them. The chaplains talked among themselves about notifying the widows.

"Who's going to McManus?" an auburn-haired priest asked quietly.

Another priest raised his hand.

"Who's going with you?" the auburn-haired priest asked.

A man in civilian clothes, wearing a Fire Department badge, raised his hand.

"Are there children involved?" the auburn-haired priest asked.

"Two," somebody said.

The priest shook his head. On one of the slips in his hand was the name of Charles Bouton of Farmingdale, L.I. The slip said that Bouton had six children.

The chaplains then pulled away, in cars with sirens sounding in the oppressive day, to notify women officially that they had become widows.

William O'Connor, whose wife had followed him to the fire, lived on the top floor of an apartment house at 79 Prospect Park Southwest. Late in the afternoon, a child's stroller was in the hallway outside the apartment, but there was no answer at the door.

Downstairs, a woman walking in with her children was asked if she knew the family.

"O'Connor? Sure, top floor. You mean the one was a cop?"

"No, he's a fireman."

"That's him. He was a cop, but he just switched over to the Fire Department six, seven months ago. Better job, a fireman He's not home? Can I do anything t help?"

"I'm afraid not," she was told.

XXXXXXXXXXXXXXXXXXXXXXXXXXXXXXXXXXXXXXXXXXXXXXXXX

4   ★☆☆☆   ○   DAILY NEWS, FRIDAY, AUGUST 4, 1978

Flame Is Always There... Waiting

PETE HAMILL

There are no safe houses.

You can leave the South Bronx. You can get out of Bushwick. You can transfer out of Brownsville and say goodby to Williamsburg. You can go to a neighborhood where the streets are lined with trees and there are no tenements waiting for the arsonist's torch. You can be far from the city of decay and collapse.

But if you are a fireman in the City of New York, there are no safe houses.

Ladder Co. 156 was not a safe house for William O'Connor, or Charles Bouton or James Cutillo. At 3:15 yesterday morning, the house was very quiet. A single fireman was on duty near the door, sipping a weak cup of coffee. Outside, a steady drizzle fell on E. 14th St., near Kings Highway, and the front doors were open to the rain. Across the street was the Sgt. Meyer Levin post of the Jewish War Veterans. The lights were out. The lights were out in all the other houses along the quiet street. It was a nice neighborhood. It was not a combat zone.

"The men are in shock," the fireman on duty was saying. "It's unbelievable. They were here, and then .. . it's just unbelievable." He sipped the coffee and looked out at the rain. "Everybody comes up againt it on the job. You get in there, and it's all around you, and you say, hey, I might die! And then you don't and you come back to the house and wash up and you forget about it. Something like this happens, you remember the times you came close."

Earlier, before midnight, Louise O'Connor had arrived at this house, in this neighborhood that appears so serene. She was with her husband's uncle. Her husband's name was William O'Connor, and he had been a fireman for only eight months. At 29, he was the youngest of the six who had died at Waldbaum's supermarket.

"She came to empty his locker," the man on duty said. "The lockers are on the third floor on this house. And she talked about how Billy had never let her come up to the third floor, and now she was finally going up there."

In the locker room, Louise O'Connor had emptied the locker, and talked about her husband. About how he had always wanted to be a fireman, and how even when he was a transit cop, waiting for the job freeze to end, waiting to transfer to the Fire Department where his father was a captain, with 25 years on the job, even then he would run to fires. He would watch the firemen work. He would talk about what being a fireman meant, in that family where even his grandfather had raced the streets of the city, fighting smoke and flames, until death finally caught up to him, too.

"He loved this job," the fireman said. "He just loved this job."

We walked into the kitchen in the back, where he

(Continued on page 65, col. 1)

(Continued from page 4)

put on some fresh coffee. There was a TV room off to the left. A young fireman was lying on his back on a cot, staring at a rerun of an old Jack Benny show. He didn't turn to say hello; going in there seemed an invasion of privacy.

"He came here with Billy," the veteran said. "They were in school together. He's been walking around all night. He can't sleep. He can't get over what happened, I guess. He can't sleep."

There were 12 men upstairs, sleeping now, waiting for the bells. But Charles Bouton wasn't there. The night before, he had arrived at this house with a fresh crewcut. He was laughing at something that had happened, out in Farmingville, where he lived with his wife and six children. He needed that haircut, and borrowed one of the kid's bikes to pedal down to the barber shop. He hadn't been on a bike for a while, but he picked up speed, and was moving down a hill, when he braked to stop at the corner. There were no brakes. He swerved into the cross street and was almost hit by a car.

'It's Very Quiet'

"The crewcut almost cost me my life," he said that night, laughing with the other men. And now one of those who had not been at Waldbaum's was sipping his coffee and staring at the rain, saying: 'Maybe he'd of been better off it he got clipped by the car."

There are no safe houses.

The rain was falling steadily over on Avenue U, where another lone man sat at the open door of the firehouse where Ladder 153 waits to do its job. The words were the same: The men were shocked. Everybody was upstairs asleep. "It's very quiet," the man said. "Thank God." The rain was falling on Waldbaum's too, where police barriers surrounded the ruined building as if it were some vicious beast that had finally been tamed. The decorative aluminum around the edge of the roof was twisted and bent. Charred wood littered the sidewalk on Ocean Ave. A scorched case of Naturipe oranges spilled from a shattered window. Broken water pipes were running freely, and when you looked through the smashed windows, twisted beams were silhouetted against the night sky. There was no roof any more. Just this open hole, and the sky, and smell of smoke and death mixed with the rain.

'It Makes You Wonder'

Some cops were sitting in a parked patrol car on Avenue Y.

"Is that the hole that was chopped in the wall?"

"That's it," one of the cops said.

"What a bitch," a visitor said.

"It makes you wonder sometimes whether it's all worth it," one of the cops said. On the ground around

the patrol car were hundreds of crushed coffee cups left behind by the reporters and the other firemen and the other people who were all still alive. All of those people were home now, in a hundred different places. And, somewhere in the city, firemen were going into burning buildings.

Later in the morning, the rain was finished, and the trees of Prospect Park glistened in the muggy heat. Louise O'Connor was not at home in the sixth-floor apartment where she and Bill O'Connor and their three children had lived at 70 Prospect Park Southwest. Her sister was home. And the kids were home, moving around the rooms, talking, making the noises kids always make. Louise and Billy's father were in Staten Island, her sister explained. They were at the cemetery.

The rules of my trade called for me to stay there, to talk, to listen, to write down the words of grief. But I looked behind me, and saw a kid's stroller in the hall, and I mumbled an apology and left. Reporters are still essentially tourists in other people's lives, and in that moment I felt as if I'd talked to the widow of one too many firemen, I'd seen enough scorched flesh, I'd gone to enough funerals.

I went down in the elevator, and remembered an argument I'd had a few weeks ago with someone who works in the city government. This man had said that I sentimentalized firemen, that they really were overpaid, their pensions bloated, their jobs—with the exception of places like the South Bronx—made up of playing cards, drinking coffee and sleeping.

Go Tell It on the Mountain

I wished that man could go around and see the families of George Rice and James Cutillo and Charles Bouton and Harold Hastings and James McManus and William O'Connor. Only O'Connor was under 30. One was 40. One was 48. I wished that man could explain to the wives how easy their husbands' jobs had been and how overpaid they were. Yeah. Go tell it on the mountain, brother.

If six cops had been shot to death yesterday, and 24 wounded, this city would be in an uproar today. This is not to demean the job of the cop, which is dangerous and complicated on a level quite different from that of the fireman. But we do take the firemen for granted. And when they die, the politicians go to the funerals, make the conventional sounds of sorrow, and blame a blind and irrational fate. Tonight, though, when smoke begins to curl through the walls of a house, and calls are placed, and alarms raised, the firemen will be there. They'll be there to save lives. They'll be there to risk death. There is no price we can place on their presence. They'll be there. And everyone of them knows one simple thing: There are no safe houses.

XXXXX   XXXX

Traditional hanging of mourning drapes.

News photo by Ed Molinari, 8/3/78. "(c) New York Daily News, used with permission."

XXXXXXXXXXXXXXXXXXXXXXXXXXXXXXXXXXXXXXXXXXXXXXXXXXXXXXXXXXXXXXXXX

For Firemen, Sadness Is a Part of the Job

By PRANAY GUPTE

When an emergency call came in at 12:40 yesterday afternoon at Ladder Company 153 in Brooklyn, Lieut. Ray Jones of the Fire Department summoned his men, threw on his helmet and coat, climbed aboard a fire engine and directed the driver to the scene.

At least 10 times a day, the lieutenant and his men set out in such a fashion, and yesterday, although each man felt a special sadness and struggled in varying ways to cope with it, the routine of work was the same.

"It's conditioning, it's an attitude the guys have on the job," Lieutenant Jones said after the men had returned from the call, which turned out to be a false alarm. "You go out on a job and you come back and you are ready to go out again. You have to be ready to go out again even if you have just lost two men who were your friends."

The words did not come easily. Firemen are generally a lively lot in the cramped confines of their firehouses — but they are not talkative about their feelings with outsiders, and the deaths in Wednesday's fire of James P. McManus and George S. Rice, both of Ladder Company 153 in the Gravesend section of Brooklyn, drew troubled responses from their colleagues. Some of the men, like Edward Smith, clearly had wept; others, like Robert Dwyer, fought hard not to.

Recalls Deaths in '66 Blaze

In a job where men have to work closely with one another and develop close friendships, Bob Dwyer was Georgie Rice's closest friend. Twelve years ago, another friend, Jimmy Gallanaugh, also a fireman, died in the great Madison Square blaze along with 11 other firefighters. Yesterday, Mr. Dwyer recalled that terrible day.

"I tell you, I walked around for months after that, I didn't believe it," he said. "Just couldn't accept it. I figured that one of these days I would get a phone call that it was an error. It wasn't easy to accept Jimmy Gallanaugh's death. And I ain't going to forget Jimmy McManus and Georgie Rice, but it will be a while before you realize it has happened."

"You don't tell a guy you love him — but you do, it's that kind of business," Mr. Dwyer said. "They're dead now, what can you do? It's like losing part of your family. Eventually, like everything else, you get over it. But right now it really hurts."

Ed Smith, a lieutenant, stood leaning against a fire engine. He was among the first officers at the scene of the blaze.

"You always think like those guys in the Army who're under fire — that it will be someone else but not me," Mr. Smith said. "Something like this only solidifies my feelings about this job : when I joined the department, I planned to retire at the end of 20 years when one can get full pension. I seriously want to get out when that time comes. Anyone wanting to stay on is seriously pushing his luck."

The New York Times •

Outside City Hall, flag flew at half-staff in honor of the dead firemen.

Lieutenant Smith looked at Fireman Dwyer and the two men silently nodded at each other. The lieutenant then stepped out of the firehouse at 901 Avenue U, looked up briefly at the black-and-purple bunting that festooned the huge doorway in mourning, and walked out into the sunshine that bathed the maples and sycamores of the street. He was headed home for the first time in nearly 24 hours.

Another Company in Mourning

Lieutenant Smith's home was two or three blocks away from Ladder Company 156 in the East Flatbush section of Brooklyn, where firemen were also mourning yesterday for three colleagues who died in the Wednesday fire: Charles S. Boutan, William O'Connor and James E. Cutillo. As at Ladder Company 153, there was black-and-purple bunting at No. 156, and the flag was at half-mast. Men stood in small clusters at the entrance, taking in the sun. Upstairs, in small dormitory-like quarters, other men also relaxed.

Jim Sobers, a fireman, was showing two neighborhood youths around the firehouse. The youths smiled gleefully as they clambered aboard a large fire engine, but Mr. Sobers was somber.

"You know,"he said, "the moment I knew they were dead — right away you visualize these guys as they were the last time you saw them.

"I still keep on thinking, 'Maybe it was a mistake.' But I know it is no mistake. I know they're gone."

Thinking About the Risks

"It's something that makes you think deeply about the business," Mr. Sobers said. "You think about the risks. At the back of your mind, those tiny everyday details begin to get large."

"Yes," Lieut. Cecil Kent said. "Yes. Take roofs, for instance. Everyone knows we can't avoid roofs in our job. But I think we're going to run scared of roofs for a while."

"We're not overly religious type of guys," the lieutenant said. "But maybe most men figure it was the will of God. How else can you begin to accept what happened?"

A few moments later, an emergency call came in. Men were summoned, helmets and coats were donned, fire engines were started, and the firefighters were off on yet another job.

XXXXXXXXXXXXXXXXXXXXXXXXXXXXXXXXXXXXXXXXXXXXXXXXXXXXXXXXXXXXXXXXXXXXXXXX

Photo credit: Neal Boenzi/NYT Pictures

Photo credit: Neal Boenzi/NYT Pictures
"Copyright (c) 1978 by The New York Times Co. Reprinted by permission."

95

Photo credit: Carl T. Gossett/NYT Pictures, 8/2/78.

XXXXXXXXXXXXXXXXXXXXXXXXXXXXXXXXXXXXXXXXXXXXXXXXXXXXXXXXXXXXXXXXXXXXX

A trip to the hearts of the fire

By
Murray Kempton

It would, of course, have been rather less messy if Mrs. George Rice had not needed to go to the heart of the fire. But, then, she was the wife of a fireman; and the rush to the heart of the fire is the soul of the fireman's covenant.

She had been driving from Islip for three hours with the friend who had brought her the news and had been unable to bring her its most important detail.

There was a war in her eyes to go on awhile being a searcher's and not yet becoming a victim's. She was almost running, and her eyes ran even faster from fireman to fireman, not really expecting, hardly even hoping, but still refusing to cease trying to find him for whom they searched. It would have taken the hardest of eyes to look at those eyes and not feel like a violator's.

No one in uniform had the heart to intercept Mrs. Rice. She came at last to the heart of what was left of the fire, the ladder where a fireman stood morosely sedating its embers. Six men dead to save an empty supermarket. The thought of such a loss for such a stake does not diminish their glory; they would, after all, have died just as serenely to save a baby if that had been their appointed task.

She called up to this last fireman with a job left to do in that place, and asked him if he had seen George Rice. He answered that he hadn't and her eyes and her feet went back to their scurryings on the street.

Five, six, maybe seven more minutes went by before the Fire Commissioner could bring himself to tell her, and there by that horrid ruin, beneath the smoke of what soon be its ashes, she began to cry out, with all those strangers looking at her; and those sodden, saddened clumps of men came suddenly together, fierce as a tribe protecting its most precious talisman, and almost drove the crowd out of the path to the ambulance and the shelter of a private grief.

A policeman had been saying earlier that when part of the roof fell, the firemen on the surviving

Quote

We cannot understand firemen; they have risen to some place among the inexplicable beauties of life.

portion had jumped to the sidewalk that was maybe thirty feet below them.

"And," he said, "the first thing the ones who could walk did was to turn around and go right back into that fire." The men who could do that without a mini-second's thought did not know how to harden themselves to tell a fireman's wife that she was a widow.

"Telling the family," said Tom McGarty of the Uniformed Fire Officers Association, "is the hardest job this department has."

He had just come back from going with a department chaplain to tell Mrs. William O'Connor. Mrs. O'Connor and her three children did not need to be told; they had seen the roof fall in. William O'Connor was a probationer; he had been a policeman for the six years while he waited for the hiring list to open again. His grandfather was a retired fireman; and his father an active one at this scene. Mrs. O'Connor had driven down to Ladder Company 156 and was waiting for his shift to end when the alarm signal sounded. He went off in his hook-and-ladder and Mrs. O'Connor followed him, so the children could see a fire. He was going up the ladder when she got there; and, as he got to the roof, he slipped and, when he had recovered his feet, he waved to his family to show that he was all right, and went to the heart of the fire.

When McGarty got to the part about Probationer O'Connor's waving, he stopped, because he had to cry again.

They are wrong who tell you that the brave don't cry. We cannot finally understand firemen; they have risen to some place among the inexplicable beauties of life. Those of the survivors who could seemed almost to need to report back to their companies yesterday afternoon. To try and talk to them seemed an intrusion beyond the call of such duty as any other sort of job could command. One of the returned paused at the door to say goodbye to a wife plainly desperate, in the quietest way, never again to let him out of her sight. He had his arm in a sling, and one of his comrades asked him how it felt.

"Least of my worries," he answered. And the mind ran to Mrs. George Rice out there in Islip, from which she had had to drive three hours to find out the worst thing she will ever hear. It has been said that if more firemen lived in this city, they would care about it more. I have a little trouble imagining to what farther degree a fireman could show how he cares about this city. For all the likes of me, men like these can live where they choose; it seems rather more to the point that they have also chosen in their offhand, unvainglorious glory, to live too few years than they ought to.

From The New York Post, 8/3/78. Reprinted with permission.

XXXXXXXXXXXXXXXXXXXXXXXXXXXXXXXXXXXXXXXXXXXXXXXXXXXXXXXXXXXXXXXXXXXXXXXXXX

NEW YORK POST, THURSDAY, AUGUST 3, 1978

The day of the chaplains: 'A sense of helplessness'

By PATRICK SULLIVAN

Yesterday the Rev. Thomas Brady, a Fire Dept. chaplain, crawled through a blazing Brooklyn supermarket assisting injured men, exhorting others to keep up their frantic efforts to find trapped comrades and ultimately annointing the six dead firefighters.

After that he and other chaplains had to break the news to the families of the victims.

"You never get used to it," Brady said. "There is very little to say, they know as soon as you walk in."

In a sense, yesterday's events could be seen as the day of the chaplains, the day their training is most needed.

"On a day like that it becomes evident, clear and tragic," Brady said. "This is when it all comes together."

Being a fire chaplain, the Rev. Alfred C. Thompson said, "is a lot like being a chaplain in the military. You know there are certain risks for the men and you hope against hope but you know you will have to go through it again."

Thompson and Brady were at the yesterday's fire — the worst since 12 firefighters died on 23rd Street in 1966 — just as the roof collapsed.

At such a frantic scene, Brady said "there is a great sense of helplessness. You try to keep the rescuers going — and try to stop the injured from going back in.

"Some went in and out that should not have gone in a second time and ended up going in three or four times," he said.

The next step, going to the victim's homes, Thompson said "is a lousy job."

Brady said, "There is no particular way to deal with it, each family seems to react differently."

Msgr. Stanislaus Jablonski said, "My case was a very sad one. I gave a little talk to the (five) children (of Fireman Charles Bouton) and the kids understood.

"Their mother told me their father had prepared them. They all cried, even the littlest one."

From The New York Post, 8/3/78. Reprinted with permission.

XXXXXXXXXXXXXXXXXXXXXXXXXXXXXXXXXXXXXXXXXXXXXXXXXXXXXXXXXXXXXXXXXXXXX

XX

Relatives Told The Sad News At a Firehouse

NY TIMES AUG. 3RD

By HOWARD BLUM

The blond, long-haired youth pulls his souped-up Pontiac to an abrupt halt in front of the red doors of the firehouse on Geritsen Avenue in Brooklyn and, despite his crutches, rushes toward a uniformed fireman.

"I hate to ask, but I'm looking for George Rice," the youth says haltingly.

"No Rice here," the fireman answers immediately. "Wait a minute, did they send you here?"

The teen-ager nods.

"You better come in here," the fireman says in a soft voice. He puts an arm around the youth's shoulder and, with his free hand, he motions to Deputy Fire Commissioner Stephen J. Murphy.

Solace Is Rejected

The deputy commissioner, after taking a name from the boy, checks six small white pieces of paper that he is clenching in his hand. Then, quiet words, almost whispers, are spoken by Deputy Commissioner Murphy. The youth learns his brother-in-law is dead.

"Oh no!" the youth shouts at the top of his lungs. Both his crutches crash to the ground.

"Oh no," he repeats, rubbing the hair off his forehead and lifting his face to the sky. Then, quickly he grabs his crutches. A fireman tries to help him, but the youth pushes him away.

"This job stinks!" the youth screams as he hobbles to his car, his right leg

Continued on Page A16, Column 3

Continued From Page A1

covered with a white plaster cast.

"The job stinks," he repeats.

Getting into his car, he yells again: "The job stinks!"

"Shut up!" Deputy Commissioner Murphy calls back at him.

Then, leaving a track of rubber behind him, the youth screeches off in his car.

The deputy commissioner, a short, white-haired man wearing thick, dark glasses and a carefully pressed brown suit, continues to stand in front of the firehouse, home base for Engine Company 321. Just three hours earlier, at about 9 A.M., each of the firemen whose names are now written on the six pieces of paper he is holding was standing on the roof of the Waldbaum's supermarket on Avenue Y. Suddenly, with a loud roar, the roof crumbled.

Deputy Commissioner Murphy arrived at the supermarket about 15 minutes later, and now he is in charge of notifying the families of the dead men.

Chaplains Are Notified

Inside the firehouse, firemen in blue uniforms are manning the telephones as relatives of the 150 men at the fire are calling to find out the fate of their loved ones. And firemen from the 321 company are calling to find fire chaplains to notify the six families.

Minutes after the boy drives off, Fire Chaplain Alfred Thompson arrives. Earlier that morning he was dressed in a white fire helmet, a black rubber coat and boots as he went into the flaming supermarket and anointed the six dead firemen. Now he has showered and changed his clothes.

The chaplain and Deputy Commissioner Murphy are joined by a circle of men from the firemen's union. While the chaplain is given a white piece of paper, a fireman yells: "Does Hastings have any children? Anyone know his wife's name?" The chaplain folds the white slip once, then twice and puts it in his wallet as if to hide it from his sight and mind.

Suddenly there is a commotion at the front of the firehouse.

"I just want to know if my brother. . ." a woman with red hair is saying through tears.

"Maureen! Maureen!" shouts a fireman rushing from the circle of men around the deputy commissioner.

"Oh Frankie, oh Frankie, you're alive," she says and then breaks into full tears as she hugs her brother-in-law.

Meanwhile, the fireman who is to accompany Chaplain Thompson to the Hastings residence has changed into a clean white shirt.

"I don't want to go," the fireman in the white shirt complains to Deputy Commissioner Murphy.

"You're a big boy," the deputy commissioner tells him. "I did this 17 times in one year."

And then the Deputy Commissioner walks away, standing alone in the front of the firehouse, still holding his pieces of white paper.

"Copyright (c) 1978 by The New York Times Company. Reprinted by permission."

XXXXXXXXXXXXXXXXXXXXXXXXXXXXXXXXXXXXXXXXXXXXXXXXXXXXXXXXXXXXX

DAILY NEWS, SUNDAY, AUGUST 6, 1978 ☆☆ 3

Thousands at 2 Firemen's Masses

By ALBERT DAVILA and DONALD SINGLETON

Thousands of firefighters from across the nation gathered yesterday morning to bury two of the six firemen killed in last Wednesday's Brooklyn supermarket blaze.

They came from Los Angeles, Chicago and Detroit, and they joined phalanxes of dignitaries at Catholic churches on Staten Island and Long Island. They stood in solemn ranks under drizzly, low-hanging gray clouds as the bodies of Fireman James McManus, 44, and Fire Lt. James E. Cutillo, 39, arrived on honor-guarded fire engines.

Rites Tomorrow For 4 Firemen

Four more firemen's funerals remain after last week's tragic Brooklyn supermarket fire. The schedule of Masses is as follows:

Harold Hastings—9:30 a.m. tomorrow in Holy Family Church, Fordham Ave. and Newbridge Road, Hicksville, L.I.

William O'Connor—10 a.m. tomorrow in Holy Name of Jesus Church, 245 Prospect Park West, Brooklyn.

George Rice—10 a.m. tomorrow in Resurrection Church, 2325 Gerritsen Ave., Brooklyn.

Charles Bouton—11:30 a.m tomorrow in St. Margaret of Scotland Church, College Road, Selden, L.I.

Mayor Koch, Gov. Carey. Fire Commissioner Augustus Beekman and several other public officials joined 3,000 firemen — including one firefighter on a visit from a suburb of Cologne, West Germany — at the Mass of the Resurrection offered for McManus at 11 a.m. in St. Adalbert's Church, 30 St. Adalbert Place, Elm Park, Staten Island.

Tears and Grief

"All I can say is that this is a tim when there are many tears and muc

Is the fire department undermanned? Read an analysis of the critical staffing situation in View, Page 48.

grief," said Koch. "I join Mayor Koch in mourning this severe loss," added Carey.

The modernistic church where McManus worshiped was packed, leaving hundreds of other mourners outside. McManus' widow, Barbara, and two daughters, Caroline, 13, and Tara, 9, sat in front pews as the flag-draped casket arrived atop a fire pumper marked with the number 153—McManus'

News photo by Tony Pescatore

Gov. Carey, Mayor Koch and Fire Commissioner Beekman pay respects to family of Fireman James McManus after rites in St. Adalbert's, S.I.

fire company — and accompanied by four men playing a dirge on muffled drums.

At the Mass, the Rev. Edward J. Dobransky, former pastor of the church, called McManus "quiet and gentle and strong."

"Perhaps what he never said in life

we can hear him say now — 'My fellow firemen, please do not see my death as useless. Each one of us knows that we face death at every alarm we answer. We are firemen because we believe in what we do. I am proud that my death

(Continued on page 37, col. 1)

(Continued from page 3)

was in the line of duty, in doing what I believed in, and have dedicated myself to all these years,'" the Rev. Dobransky said.

After the Mass had ended, a bugler sounded taps.

The scene was similar at St. Luke's Church in Brentwood, L.I., where First Deputy New York City Fire Commissioner Stephen Murphy led more than 1,000 firemen gathered for the Mass offered for Lt. Cutillo.

Cutillo's widow, Evelyn, and the couple's two adopted children, Gina, 12, and James, 9, sat in front pews as the eulogy was delivered by the Rev. Thomas Brady, a New York City Fire Department chaplain who was present at the scene of the fatal blaze in a Waldbaum's supermarket in Sheepshead Bay, Brooklyn.

The Rev. Brady made reference to a scene from the movie, "To Kill a Mockingbird." In the film, a white attorney had bravely represented a black defendant in a southern court; the attorney's child is told afterward, "Stand up, your father's passing by."

Addressing Cutillo's children, the Rev. Brady said, "We stand today because your father is passing by." Most of the people in the church wept.

Following the Mass, there was a procession of 20 fire engines to the Northport (L.I.) Rural Cemetery 10 miles away.

News photo by T. Pescatore, 8/5/78. "(c) New York Daily News, used with permission."

XXXXXXXXXXXXXXXXXXXXXXXXXXXXXXXXXXXXXXXXXXXXXXXXXXXXXXXXXXXXXXXXXXXXX

DAILY NEWS, SUNDAY, AUGUST 6, 1978

News photo by Jim Hughes

Kin, Comrades Mourn Dead Firemen

Casket of James McManus is carried to waiting fire truck after funeral yesterday at St. Adalbert's Church, Staten Island. Rites also were held yesterday for Lt. James Cutillo at St. Luke's Church, Brentwood, L.I. Both firefighters were killed when roof of a Brooklyn supermarket collapsed during a fire Wednesday. Firemen from across the country converged on New York for the two funerals, joining family, friends and local politicians and dignitaries in mourning the two fallen firefighters. Funerals will be held Monday for the other four firemen killed in the fire.

Story on page 3

News photo by Jim Hughes, 8/5/78.
"(c) New York Daily News, used with permission."

XXXXXXXXXXXXXXXXXXXXXXXXXXXXXXXXXXXXXXXXXXXXXXXXXXXXXXXXXXXXXXX

101

Photo credit: Edward Hausner/NYT Pictures, 8/5/78:

Family of Lt. James Cutillo arrives at St. Luke's Church.

Long blue line of firefighters enters St. Luke's Church, Brentwood, L.I., for funeral of comrade, Lt. James Cutillo.

News photo by Gordon Rynders, 8/5/78. "(c) New York Daily News, used with permission."

XXXXXXXXXXXXXXXXXXXXXXXXXXXXXXXXXXXXXXXXXXXXXXXXXXXXXXXXXXXXXXXXXXXXXX

XXXXXXXXXXXXXXXXXXXXXXXXXX

Thousands Turn Out At Rites for 2 Firemen Killed by Falling Roof

By DENA KLEIMAN

Thousands of firefighters, public officials and others turned out in the rain yesterday for the first of the funerals for six firefighters who perished last Wednesday when a blazing roof collapsed at a Brooklyn supermarket.

The ceremonies yesterday were held in Brentwood, L.I., for Lieut. James E. Cutillo, 39 years old, and in the Elm Park section of Staten Island for James P. McManus, 45.

At each, throngs of uniformed firefighters stood at attention as the coffin of their fallen colleague was hoisted onto a firetruck. Taps were sounded and the coffin was led slowly past the ranks to the solemn beat of a requiem drum. Many wept.

Both funerals attracted firefighters from throughout the city, the friends and families of the victims and the friends and families of other firefighters who have died in the line of duty over the years. Although most had not known the dead firefighters personally, many said that they shared the grief because tragedy potentially faced every firefighter's family.

"I don't like funerals because it makes

Continued on Page 28, Column 1

Continued From Page 1

me realize the position my family would be in if it ever happened to me," said Robert Lind, a firefighter from Staten Island, who attended the rites for Mr. McManus.

"I don't want it to happen to my father," said Michael Sottile Jr., the 13-year-old son of a Bronx firefighter, who accompanied his father at the funeral for Mr. Cutillo.

The funerals for the four other firefighters who died in the Waldbaum's supermarket blaze — Charles S. Boutan, Harold F. Hastings, William O'Connor and George S. Rice — are scheduled to take place tomorrow.

The funeral for Mr. McManus, which took place at St. Adalbert's Roman Catholic Church on Staten Island attracted the top public officials and Fire Department representatives. Mayor Koch and Governor Carey attended, as well as Fire Commissioner Augustus A. Beekman.

"Perhaps we should let Jim McManus speak in his own quiet but strong way," said the Rev. Edward J. Dobransky, who conducted the ceremony and has been a close friend of the firefighter's family. "Perhaps what he never said in life we can hear him say now." Father Dobransky then paraphrased what he said Mr. McManus might have told his colleagues: "Please do not see my death as useless. Each one of us knows that we face death at every alarm we answer. We are firemen because we believe in what we do. I am proud that my death was in the line of duty."

Mr. McManus, who lived in Graniteville, S.I., had been a firefighter for 17 years.

'I Weep and Grieve'

During the funeral rite, Mr. McManus's mother, Eliabeth, his wife, Barbara, and two daughters Tara, 9 years old and Caroline, 13, sat in the first pew of the crowded church. They clung to each other as the clergyman spoke. Mr. Carey and Mr. Koch walked over to them and offered their condolences. Mr. Koch leaned over and kissed the fireman's widow.

"There is really very little to say," Mr. Koch told reporters afterward. "I weep

and grieve with the families of these six men."

There was no representative from the Mayor's office at the rites for Mr. Cutillo, but the funeral, was moving.

Hundreds of firefighters gathered in in front of St. Luke's Roman Catholic Church shortly after 10 A.M. A gentle rain fell as the firetruck with Mr. Cutillo's coffin slowly filed past the crowd.

The only sounds that pierced the hush were those of the heavy platform that creaked as the coffin was lowered from the truck to the street, and the wails of Mr. Cutillo's widow. A brief ceremony took place outside the church. But the candles were soon doused by the rain and the service had to be continued inside the church's entranceway.

'City Is a Cold Place'

The City of New York is a cold place," said the Rev. Thomas Brady, the Fire Department chaplain, who conducted the service. "People don't usually have time for too much thinking or too much weeping. But in the past few days it has been brought to its knees."

Mr. Cutillo's mother, Louise, his wife, Evelyn, and children, Gina, 12, and Jimmy, 9, sat in the fifth pew of the church. Their sobs echoed as Father Brady praised Mr. Cutillo's bravery.

"It is fitting and symbolic that his should be the first of the funerals," Father Brady said of Mr. Cutillo, who was the officer in charge of the men on the roof that collapsed. "That once again he should lead his men."

After the ceremony, the firefighters stood at attention outside the church, and in the heavy rain saluted the coffin as taps were played and the firetruck began its journey to Northport Rural Cemetery in Northport.

"I feel like I'm going through it all over again," said Joan Davidson of Brentwood, whose brother was killed three years ago in the line of duty. "I don't know half the men here. But they may have come for my brother. I know if my brother had been alive he'd have been here."

"I understand," someone said, in an effort to comfort Mrs. Davidson, who had begun to weep.

"No," she replied. "You really can't. No one can unless they have been through it. I feel like I'm living through it all over again, except I'm not in the limousine."

"Copyright (c) 1978 by The New York Times Company. Reprinted by permission."

XXXXXXXXXXXXXXXXXXXXXXXXXXXXXXXXXXXXXXXXXXXXXXXXXX

Irish Wake: an Exercise in Grief

NEWS AUG 6, 1978

JIMMY BRESLIN

The rain ran down the puffed, charred timber that once held up the building roof and then soaked into the hills of debris under the wood, causing the smell of the place to heighten rather than be washed away. The street sat in the odor of a thousand cellars that had just been thrown open.

Six firemen had died here last Wednesday. And the longer you remained on the sidewalk, the more grotesque the wreckage became, the more disturbing the conversation.

"They had a fire in there about 10 days ago," a man said. "Next to the men's room on the mezzanine. There was a portable closet with dirty aprons and things like that. The fire was in the base of the closet. The people working in the store discovered it and extinguished it themselves."

He Remembers a Trash Fire

Another man, holding an umbrella, said, "I know of another one myself. The Friday before Labor Day last year. I just got down from Saratoga. In the back there, along the rear wall, that's where they had the meats on one side and the milk and dairy products on the other. They had these three 55-gallon drums by the milk. Trash fires started in all three of 'em. I remember they put a security guard back there by the drums after that."

A man in civilian clothes and showing a fire marshal's badge began to talk to the one with the umbrella. I went away fighting the vision of some disturbed person lighting small fires until one of them became too big.

The wake for William O'Connor was being held in Duffy's funeral home on Ninth St. and Fourth Ave. in South Brooklyn. O'Connor was 29 and he was the one who stood on the roof of the burning building, waved to his wife and three kids in the street, and then died when the roof caved in.

To get to Duffy's you drove down Seventh Ave., where young girls, eagerly pushing womanhood, sat on the window ledges of second and third-floor apartments and called down to boys swaggering on the dirty sidewalks. In front of the Board of Health's child-care station on 16th St., a huge man in an undershirt, fat billowing, sat on a chair. His dog, an angry husky, was leashed to the light pole. The leash was long enough to allow the dog to make a pass at anybody who went by. On Ninth St., Mr. Martin Tuxedos, on the ground floor, and the two apartments over it, were gutted by fire. At the bottom of the hill stood an old Catholic fort, the tan paint peeling from the bricks. A woman said, "This is the Fourth Avenue St. Thomas. There's two St. Thomases around here, you see."

A Doubt, A Wonder

The Duffy Funeral Home was alongside the church. Inside, in a large, silent room, Louise O'Connor stood in front of the closed casket of her husband. Her father-in-law, in pain, was a step away. Hugh Carey stood with him.

"I hope God knows what he's doing." O'Connor said. This is the most, a doubt, a wonder, that most

(Continued on page 64, col. 1)

(Continued from page 3)

people in the Diocese of Brooklyn ever raise. Denial is virtually unheard of.

Carey, hands clasped in front of him, was silent. No one else answered O'Connor, either. In the religion they all learned, there is only one answer to a question like this: "Q. How do we know this to be so? A. Because it is a mystery."

"The three clidren will keep you busy," Carey said to Louise O'Conner.

"Who should know that better than you?" she said.

Louise O'Connor's uncle, Bob Regula, sat along one of the walls. "Only the other day, we were changing radios in our cars and Bill heard somebody yelling for the police. They thought they had a burglar or something, and Bill grabs a screwdriver and starts running. I say, 'What good's that?' And he says, 'This is all I need.' Now look at what we got. The kid, Billy, the 6-year-old, came up to me before. He says, 'Uncle Sandy, you know my father died? He doesn't know what it means." He shook his head." And they were going to Breezy Point when it happened."

Breezy Point is not a fashionable vacation spot. It is at the Brooklyn end of the Rockaways, a colony of small bungalows that are nerve-racking when filled with children on a rainy day. But it is the place where cops and firemen go, and when you mentioned Breezy Point at William O'Connor's wake, you were speaking of their Hamptons.

"There's No Hope"

Bill O'Connor's uncle, Phil Ruvolo, who is also a fireman, went outside for a cigaret.

"When did you find out?" he was asked.

"At the fire," he said. "I'm on a 96 when the box came in. We responded, and when I got there I went to guys I knew and said, 'Where's Angel?' That's the name we called Bill. A guy said to me, 'He was on the roof when it went.' I said, 'What part?' They guy said, 'Center.' I went in. I couldn't find anything. I came back out and called the father and told him to come down. I saw Louise, and she said to me, 'Uncle Phil, Billy's missing.' I said, 'I know. Honey. I'm looking for him.' I went back in and couldn't find anything. I came out and the father was standing there and he saw my eyes and he knew. I told him, 'There's no hope.' "

He stared at the sidewalk and then went back inside. To the curb pulled a fire truck with a seal on the front saying, "Tot Finder," and under it a picture of a fireman carrying a child out of flames. The firemen, in short-sleeve shirts. one of them with a radio over his shoulder, walked inside, to a room that was becoming crowded, but was still silent.

The men stood; and the women, fingering purses or bracelets or sweaters, but always fingering something, sat on folding chairs. There were no smiles, and nobody told stories. Everybody looked at, and then tried not to look at, the young widow who kept standing in front of this closed coffin with an American flag draped over it, and a fireman's hat sitting atop the flag. It was a wake for an Irish kid from Brooklyn but it was no different from what grieving human beings do anywhere. There is no laughter, and there never

was at an Irish wake. It's a table without foundation. For the Irish, the same as anybody else, a wake is an exercise in misery, not alcohol.

"I hate this place." Tome Gates, the fireman, said. "The last time I was in here was when Hughie McCabe got killed in Vietnam. I came in here at lunchtime, and the place was empty. I signed my name and got right out."

Firemen in White Gloves

The faces in the room became straighter and more solemn. They all seemed to imitate the two firemen in white gloves who were standing alongside in the coffin as an honor guard.

We went downstairs to smoke. The sound of people exhaling rubbed the nerves. Nobody spoke. Upstairs, at the front door, Louise O'Connor was talking to the young guy at the reception desk. He went in to the desk and brought out a bottle of aspirin. He handed her a couple, and she walked to the water cooler.

DAILY NEWS, SUNDAY, AUGUST 6, 1978

News photo by James McGrath

Mrs. William O'Connor (left) with son, and Mayor Koch (right) at Mass for Fireman William O'Connor in Brooklyn. Mrs. O'Connor and children had watched as her husband fell through blazing roof after he waved to them while fighting supermarket fire.

Fire Dept. Buries 4 More of Bravest

By GEORGE JAMES
With Gerald Kessler, Michael Hanrahan and Thomas Raftery

The flag-draped coffin was brought from the rear of the fire engine to the steps of the Church of the Resurrection in Gerritsen Beach, Brooklyn, yesterday. Four-year old Colleen Rice's plaintive voice shattered the silence and pierced the heart: "Is my father in there?"

"He's up in heaven with God," her aunt, Eileen Fennimore, told the blonde girl she held in her arms.

"Is my father going to come out?" The question went unanswered. The funeral mass for fireman George Rice began in the Romanesque-Spanish Missionary style church where George and Carol Rice were married 15 years ago.

Three Other Masses

The questioning of life and death went on at three other masses of christian burial; at the Mass for William O'Connor, 29, in the Holy Name of Jesus Church in Park Slope, Brooklyn; for Harold Hastings, 40, at Holy Family in Hicksville, L.I.; for Charles Bouton, 38, at St. Margaret of Scotland Church in Selden, L.I.

Seven thousand firemen from New

York and Long Island and from across the nation gathered to attend the Masses or to line the sweltering streets in silence. They said goodby to the last four of six firemen who died last Wednesday when a burning supermarket roof in Brooklyn collapsed.

Last Saturday, James McManus, 44, of Staten Island, and James E. Cutillo, 39, of Brentwood, L.I., were buried.

"These funerals of the six have taken on the dimension of a Greek tragedy," said Mayor Koch after attending O'Connor's funeral in Park Slope with Gov. Carey and other city officials.

At the Rice funeral, the Rev. James P. Sweeney, the celebrant, recalled he had married the Rices in this church. "When they took each other for better or for worse, the future was hidden from their eyes, but had they known of today, had they been asked if they would give up each other, their answer would have been a firm no," the Rev. Sweeney said. Rice was buried in St. Charles Cemetery, Farmingdale, L.I.

At O'Connor's funeral the Rev. Michael McGee called him a man who was always "on duty" to serve his fellow man. "As he lived in the hands of God, he died in the hands of God," said the Rev. McGee.

O'Connor was buried at the Moravian Cemetery on Staten Island.

At Hastings' funeral Mass, the Rev. Bernard J. McGrath called him "an individual who had served so well. All these ceremonies and all these words expressed in the last several days can in no sense properly meet the needs, properly size the occasion we commemorate to send the family sincere sympathy and condolences."

Hastings was buried in Long Island National Cemetery, Pinelawn.

At Bouton's funeral, the Rev. Thomas Brady, the Fire Department chaplain who gave last rites to the six firemen, encouraged Bouton's wife, Catherine, and six children to stand up in life with the courage and generosity Bouton had shown.

"The tragedy has turned people's lives around," said Brady. "Not only firefighters but so many people have now sought new meaning in their own lives, marriages and families."

Bouton was buried at Holy Sepulchre Cemetery in Coram, L.I.

News photo by James McGrath, 8/7/78. "(c) The New York Daily News, used with permission."

Fire Department's Greatest Toll: 12 Died on 23d St. 12 Years Ago

By JOSEPH B. TREASTER

NY TIMES
AUG. 3, 1978

Yesterday's death of six firemen was the city's most grievous loss of firefighters in a single incident since a dozen firemen were killed 12 years ago when a floor collapsed while they were fighting a fire in a drugstore on West 23d Street. The 12 deaths constituted the worst such tragedy ever in New York.

Last summer, four volunteers of the Eaglewood, N.J., Fire Department died in a sudden shift of wind in a forest fire, and two years earlier eight Philadelphia firemen died in an oil refinery fire. But those were exceptions, according to Arthur Washburn of the National Fire Protection Association in Boston.

"If you look at the major incidents over the years, you'll see that in the majority of multiple deaths of firemen something has collapsed," Mr. Washburn said. In yesterday's accident, the firemen were killed when the roof of a burning Brooklyn supermarket collapsed.

Last year, Mr. Washburn said, 134 firemen were reported to have died on duty across the country. About 100 of them were professional firemen, including six members of the New York City Fire Department.

One Death Earlier in Year

Until the supermarket fire there had been one fatality among New York firemen this year, a spokesman for the Uniformed Firefighters Association said. That was a fireman who died of a heart attack while fighting a blaze. In 1976, he said, nine New York firemen died in the line of duty.

All of the New York firemen who died last year, died separately, the spokesman for the association said, but three of the deaths in 1976 occurred when a roof collapsed in a restaurant fire in Queens. .

Most of the deaths elsewhere in the country last year came individually, according to Walt Lambert, the director of research for the International Association of Firefighters in Washington. Over the past decade, he added, there had been a half dozen or so multiple deaths of firemen a year.

Overall, the authorities said, the greatest cause of death among firemen — 44 percent, according to one study — is heart attacks, brought on by continuous stress, exposure to heat and smoke inhalation.

According to Mr. Washburn, the worst disaster for firemen in American history was also the country's worst industrial accident: a series of explosions and fires aboard two ships being loaded with ammonium nitrate in Texas City, Tex., about 35 miles southwest of Houston on April 16 and 17, 1947. Twenty-seven firemen were among the more than 500 persons killed. Some 3,000 others were injured.

Re: pp. 106 and 107,
"Copyright (c) 1978 by
The New York Times Co.
Reprinted by permission."

XXXXXX XXXXXXXXXXXXXXXXXXXXXXXXXXXXXXXXXXX

Hero Funerals Held for 4 Firemen, Last of 6 Killed at Brooklyn Blaze

By JOHN KIFNER

Fireman William O'Connor rode Fire Engine 156 for the last time yesterday.

His brother firefighters bore his coffin down the steps of Holy Name of Jesus Roman Catholic Church in Brooklyn to a ceremonial pumper bearing the number of the ladder truck that had carried him to the blaze that took his life.

To the muffled beat of drums, firemen bore three coffins from three other Roman Catholic churches and, under leaden skies, placed them on three fire trucks as the last of the six firemen killed last Wednesday, when the roof of a burning Brooklyn supermarket collapsed, were buried.

Out-of-Town Firemen Present

Thousands of firemen, many from other cities, attended the funerals, standing at attention in long, dark blue rows as the red fire trucks carried the flag-draped coffins away.

The six firemen died in the department's worst fire disaster in the city in a dozen years when the roof of the Waldbaum's supermarket in the Sheepshead Bay neighborhood suddenly gave way in a ball of flame and dropped the men into the heart of the fire.

Two of the men, Lieut. James E. Cutillo and Firemen James P. McManus, were buried on Saturday. The four others were buried yesterday, with the funeral of Fireman O'Connor designated as the formal, honor ceremony.

Governor Carey, Mayor Koch, Fire Commissioner Augustus A. Beekman and City Council President Carol Bellamy were among the 800 mourners who filled the pews and aisles of the 100-year-old red brick church in the Windsor Terrace neighborhood near Brooklyn's Prospect Park.

'Always on Duty'

"He died the only way that he could — that was on duty," the Rev. Michael McGee said of Fireman O'Connor, who had been a firefighter, a tradition in his family, for but seven months. "Bill was always on duty. He was always there with his laugh and his humor."

Fireman Harold Hastings, a chief's aide in the 42d Battalion, was buried after a mass at Holy Family Church in Hicksville, L.I. Fireman George S. Rice was buried after a mass at the Resurrection Roman Catholic Church in Brooklyn. And Fireman Charles S. Bouton was buried after a mass at St. Margaret of Scotland Roman Catholic Church in Selden, L.I.

"You never get used to funerals," Mayor Koch said after the service for Fireman O'Connor. "They're all very painful. The funerals of these six have taken on the dimensions of a Greek tragedy."

Fireman O'Connor's wife, Louise, and their three children sat in a front pew. Last Wednesday they had gone to his firehouse to pick him up after work for a day at the beach at Breezy Point. Instead they found that he had been called out to a fire just before his shift ended. The family drove to the fire and saw Fireman O'Connor wave jauntily to them from his ladder, then disappear as the roof collapsed.

In the front row, too, were Fireman O'-Connor's father, William, a fireman in Ladder 168, and his uncle, Philip Ruvolo, of Engine 254.

In the Gerritson Beach section of Brooklyn, the Rev. James P. Sweeny, who had officiated at the marriage of Fireman George Rice and his wife, Carol, conducted a burial mass at the Resurrection Church, where George Rice had once been an altar boy.

Like many of the city's firemen, he had moved from the old neighborhood to Long Island — Islip Terrace — but the family had lived in the middle-class Brooklyn area for as long as anyone could recall, and it seemed fitting to have the funeral service there.

Understanding a Youthful Death

"Faith is the only means of understanding such a youthful death." Father Sweeny said in his euology.

The Fire Department did not have enough chromed, polished ceremonial trucks for all the funerals, so the men of Engine Company 321 gave their battered pumper — one of the trucks used to fight the fatal blaze — two coats of fresh paint last night.

"Death is a hazard of our job," Lieut. Salvatore Augeri of Engine 321 said. "But we're not paid to die. I wish people wouldn't think that we are paid to die but would remember what firemen do to preserve life."

A lone bagpiper stood by the Holy Family Church in Hicksville as the family of Fireman Harold Hastings filed into the church behind his coffin. Some 2,000 people — many of them firemen, others neighbors — lined the streets and crowded into the church.

"It is not the first or the last time that his profession is one that will be remembered as one filled with self-sacrificing elements," the Rev. Bernard J. McGrath said, "and one which will bring forth the best sentiments human beings are capable of."

Friends of Two Victims

In Selden, L.I., 1,500 firemen, friends and neighbors of Fireman Charles S. Bouton went to St. Margaret of Scotland Church to pay their respects. Tony Stack, a city fireman in Queens and a close friend of the dead man drove the pumper truck that carried the coffin.

Fireman Stack's wife, Grace, crying outside the church, said that she and her husband were close friends not only of the Boutons but also of the family of Lieutenant Cutillo, who was buried on Saturday in Brentwood.

"I am proud of my husband," she said, "but I am sorry these men had to risk their lives for an empty building. I don't think of these things all the time, but you're never the same after a tragedy like this."

The families of the six firemen include 18 children.

N.Y. TIMES
8/8/78

XXX

Photo opposite page:
William O'Connor takes last ride on fire truck.

Credit: Paul Hosefros/NYT Pictures, 8/7/78.

Photo opposite page:
Catherine Bouton places a rose on coffin of husband, Charles.

Credit: Lou Manna/NYT Pictures, 8/7/78.

XXXXXXXXXXXXXXXXXXXXXXXXXXXXXXXXXXXXXXXXXXXXXXXXXXXXXXXXXXXXXXX

xxx

xxxxxxxxxxxxxxxxxxxxxxxxxxxxxxxxxxxxxxxxxxxxxxxxxxxxxxxxxxxxxxxxxxxxx

Funeral Mass for Firefighter George Rice has just ended.

Photo credit: Gary Settle/NYT Pictures, 8/7/78.

XXXXXXXXXXXXXXXXXXXXXXXXXXXXXXXXXXXXXXXXXXXXXXXXXXXXXXXXXXXXXXXXXXXXX

News photos by Dennis Caruso and Willie Anderson

Widow Donna Hastings and son Brian, 14, (photo left) entering Hicksville, L.I., church. At Resurrection Church in Brooklyn (photo right), Mrs. Carol Rice at husband's funeral with son Kevin and daughter Colleen, held by Mrs. Rice's sister, Eileen Fennimore.

A Fire That's Burned in His Memory

By THOMAS RAFTERY

Etched on Bill Kelly's forehead is a scar showing four stitches. His nose is still scabbed from the burns he received. He will never forget the day his wife almost became a widow and his four kids almost became fatherless.

"Death, be not proud," Kelly muttered yesterday. Kelly had plunged through the middle of the roof of a Sheepshead Bay supermarket last Wednesday and was lucky to live to tell about it.

Kelly was sipping coffee along with 800 other firemen who attended the funeral at the Church of the Resurrection in Gerritsen Beach, Brooklyn, of fireman George Rice, who was killed when the supermarket roof collapsed.

"I was in the center of the building with a hose line," recalled Kelly, a

Where to Send Family Gifts

Contributions to the families of six firemen killed in the Brooklyn supermarket blaze, last week may be sent to either of two funds:

● Family Fund, FDNY, c/o First Deputy Fire Commissioner Stephen J. Murphy, 110 Church St., New York, N.Y., 10007.

● The Aug. 2 Firefighters & Widows and Children's Fund, P.O. Box 1800, Brooklyn, N.Y., 11202.

member of Engine Company 246. "Fire was breaking through the roof. We tried to keep it back, then there was a little ripple effect and the roof gave way."

Kelly plunged through the roof and attic flooring of the store. Unlike many of the men who were then hung up in the attic flooring, where smoke and flames engulfed them, he plummeted to the main level.

Kelly saw a tunnel, created by debris stacked up along a line of refrigerators.

Then Kelly crawled out. He said he could feel the suction trying to pull him back as flames leaped into the sky. He was beyond hearing the cries of fellow firefighters who were caught in the rafters before being dashed to the ground, when he passed out near a store window.

Kelly, 44, and an 18-year veteran of the department, was dragged out of the store and sent to the hospital in an Emergency Medical Service ambulance.

Photos by D. Caruso and W. Anderson, 8/7/78. "(c) The New York Daily News, used with permission"

XXXXXXXXXXXXXXXXXXXXXXXXXXXXXXXXXXXXXXXXXXXXXXXXXXXXXXXXXXXXXXXXXXXXXXX

Two Firefighters Eulogized in Brooklyn
'A Man Who Always Went Out of His Way to Be Helpful'

By MATTHEW MONAHAN

Fireman George Rice, "a man who always went out of his way to be helpful," was buried Monday after services at Resurrection Church, Brooklyn, the same place where he and his wife Carol were married in 1963.

Rice, 38, was a member of Ladder Co. 153, Brooklyn. The 13-year veteran of the Department died Aug. 2 with five other firemen while fighting a supermarket blaze. It was his first day back to work after vacation.

The slow-moving cortege followed a Fire Department Member who played a drum dirge and red pumper truck which bore Rice's flag-draped casket.

Under overcast skies, more than 700 colleagues from New York and other communities stood four-deep along a block-long stretch of Gerritsen Ave. that was closed to traffic. Wearing white gloves, they saluted as Rice's remains were gently transferred from the truck to the church. The 1,000-seat Spanish Mission-Romanesque church was filled to capacity by firemen, family members, friends, parishioners and strangers who wanted to pay their respects.

Mourners were met by Bishop Charles Mulrooney, who presided at the Mass of Christian Burial. He was accompanied by concelebrants: Fr. Raymond Shevlin, pastor; Fr. James P. Sweeney chaplain at Flushing Hospital, who married the Rices when he was assigned to Resurrection, and Fr. Terrence Mulkerin, a long-time family friend.

"Mommy's All Right"

Looking drawn, Mrs. Rice wore a simple black dress with two Fire Department lapel pins attached. She led her adopted children into church. In what seemed to be answers to inaudible questions, Mrs. Rice told Kevin, 8, and Colleen, 4, "Mommy's all right. We'll be going home soon." She bent over, kissed her son and, flanked by relatives, walked down the center aisle.

In his homily, Fr. Sweeney said "On this same spot Carol and George discussed part of the future to which they were pledging themselves and a part hidden from their eyes. He was the kind of man who frequently put hard work over his own ease, duty over his safety.

"We offer sympathy to George's family, parents, comrades and friends. We commend him to God's care and to the Sacred Heart of Jesus, the source of all consolation.

"We give him back to you, Oh God, Who gave him to us. As You did not lose in his giving, so we do not lose in his return."

Readings were done by Terence Medican, Mrs. Rice's brother, and Fireman Anthony Dragonetti of Engine Co. 254, Rice's companion unit. James Rice, brother of the late fireman, read the prayers of the faithful. Parents James and Mary Rice came back from their retirement home in Florida. The elder Rice was a fireman.

Before Mass, Bishop Mulrooney was introduced to Mary Campbell, whose husband Terence, a fireman, was injured in the blaze that claimed Rice and the others. The Bishop assured her "We are praying for your husband." And Mrs. Campbell, holding his hands, said "That will pull him through. God is good."

Other Parishioners Hurt

Campbell and his family are members of Resurrection parish as are Lieut. Joseph Shea and Fireman William Yard, who were also injured in the fire. Campbell is still hospitalized and the latter two have been released.

Bishop Mulrooney, representing Bishop Mugavero, who was out of the country, said "It is very fitting that the Diocese be represented here. We are expressing our feelings of this tragedy through a Mass, to support each other and to let the family know they are not alone. The accent is placed on new life and eternal salvation, which George Rice achieved early."

Fr. Shevlin remembered Rice as a youngster. "He was a very conscientious kid. As an altar boy he helped the others learn Latin." Rice, one of six children, lived with his wife and children in Islip Terrace, L.I. Mrs. Rice is a native of nearby Good Shepherd parish.

Rice's willingness to assist those in need and his manner were recalled by Fr. Mulkerin, who grew up with James Rice. "George always went out of his way to be helpful. He was a cheerful, though a quiet person."

Fireman Dragonetti worked with Rice. "George was a good fireman who did his job to the utmost. He could take a joke. In a firehouse the guys form a tight-knit family. You work, eat, talk and kid-around together. When tragedy strikes the loss is very heavy. There is no guarantee that when you go out on a call that you'll return," he said somberly.

After Mass the congregation moved outside. Traffic at Gerritsen and Whitney Aves. came to a halt as a bugler played Taps. The assembled firemen gave a final salute and the procession drove to St. Charles Cemetery, Farmingdale, for the burial.

From The Tablet, 8/10/78.

XXXXXXXXXXXXXXXXXXXXXXXXXXXXXXXXXXXXXXXXXXXXXXXXXXXXXXXXXXXXXXXXXXX

XX

'He Died the Only Way He Could . . . He Was Always on Duty'

BY DORENE REARDON

Two firemen sat quietly in the waiting room of Duffy's Funeral Home. Relatives, friends and fellow officers filed past them down the corridor which led to chapel D, where William O'Connor was.

"How did your wife react?" one finally asked.

"She took it bad, real bad," came the reply.

William O'Connor was one of six fire fighters who died last week when the roof of a burning supermarket collapsed. He was 29 years old and a fireman for just eight months.

Ten minutes after the cave-in, Fire Chaplain Thomas Brady arrived on the scene. "In the beginning there was a lot of confusion about who was lost and who wasn't," recalled Fr. Brady, who is also the dean of studies at Cathedral Prep, Brooklyn. He immediately donned firefighting apparel and went into the rubble as 50 other men attempted to rescue those trapped. "It was an hour and a half before they were all found. I administered the last rites in the building before they were carried out to ambulances.

With Louise O'Connor and other distraught wives waiting on the streets for word about their husbands, Fr. Bardy's next task was just as difficult. "There are no great words of wisdom that can be uttered at a time like that," he said. "You simply hold onto the people."

For years, Mrs. O'Connor had been reaching out to help those in trouble as head of the Volunteer Homemaking Program in her parish. Now it was time for someone to reach out for her.

From The Tablet, 8/10/78.

XXXXXXXXXXXXXXXXXXXXXXXX

Active Parishioners

The O'Connors are parishioners of Holy Name, Brooklyn, in the trust sense of the word. "Both Billy and Louise went to the parish grammar school," said Father Michael McGee. "But more importantly, they were both very active here. Billy was working on the Bishop's Diocesan Fundraising Committee. Earlier he helped me on recollection days with the teenagers.

"Louis literally runs the Homemakers Program. She is always at the rectory making sure the volunteers visit the people in the community who need help. Whether they were just released from the hospital or were homebound, Louise made sure their needs were met."

William O'Connor's family has a proud history of men who served in the Fire Department. His father Harry is a Captain and his grandfather was also a fireman who was killed in a blaze. Phil Ruvolo, was assigned to the same fire as his nephew. When news of the death was announced, Ruvolo left the burning building to take Louise O'Connor home. His son, Phil Ruvolo, Jr., who was a lector at O'Connor's funeral, will become a fireman in three weeks.

"Billy lived to be a fireman," recalled Father McGee. "After his discharge from the Navy, he was a little down when he didn't get into the department. He became a Transit Policeman and then eight months ago his name came up and he joined the Fire Department.

"At that point he had everything he ever wanted. He was good to his family and in fact to everyone. He was somebody who was always ready to help anyone of his neighbors."

"I remember when the first anniversary of my ordination was approaching; Billy and Louise invited me to their house to say Mass. They were two very special individuals."

That sentiment was echoed by Father John Gildea of Holy Name. "I've known Billy and Louise for the three years I've been here. I probably knew them better than most parishioners because they were the kind of people always involved in community affairs.

"Anytime there was a neighborhood meeting, Billy would attend if his schedule permitted. He was an outspoken guy who didn't hesitate when giving his opinions. I think in most cases his opinion was right."

William O'Connor's concern for others extended from his family, to his neighbors and to his fellow officers who nicknamed him Angel. "He made a big impression on everyone he met," said Father McGee. "Louise's father is in a wheelchair and is homebound. Billy would spend hours with him, just talking about everyday things. He was just a tremendous individual

"He lived for his family and to be a fireman. Louise's consolation and her peace comes from the fact that he was doing what he wanted to do. And he was so happy doing it."

At the Mass politicians and firemen from throughout the East Coast were in attendance. But the Church and streets were also filled with those whose lives had been touched by William O'Connor. Chief celebrant was Father Richard Beliveau with priests from both Holy Name and neighboring parish Immaculate Heart of Mary con-celebrating, and Bishop John J. Synder presiding.

In a barely audible tones John Fairbanks delivered one of the readings, suppressing the emotions that almost overwhelmed him. Fairbanks had flown into New York as soon as word reached him that his best friend since childhood had died.

Always on Duty

Father McGee as homilist said "Billy died the only way he could - on duty, because he was always on duty. He was always there to help. Billy knew what it meant to serve his fellow man. He knew what it meant to love...

"He had what most men have - a dream. And that dream did not die in the fire. Don't let it be said that he died in vain because all life in the hands of God is precious.

"Billy had the gift of life and lived it to the fullest. I say to Billy 'Thank you for helping me to appreciate the gift of life'."

As the Mass concluded Bishop Synder gave the final blessing. Quietly he approached the young widow and her three small children. There were soft-spoken intimate words between them and then with O'Connor's parents.

As the congregation rose for the recessional hymn, six firemen escorted William O'Connor out of Holy Name Church for the last time. Outside fire contingents stood at attention as their fellow officer was raised to the top of a blazing red fire truck while the sound of Taps echoed throughout the streets of Park Slope

113

**Firefighter 1st Grade
CHARLES S. BOUTON**

assigned to Ladder Co. 156 . . . appointed to Department September 14, 1968 . . . married . . .

. . . children — 6 . . . age 38.

**Firefighter 1st Grade
HAROLD F. HASTINGS**

assigned Battalion 42 . . . appointed to Department October 6, 1962 . . . married . . .

children — 3 . . . age 39.

**Firefighter 1st Grade
JAMES P. McMANUS**

assigned to Ladder Co. 153 . . . appointed to Department February 11, 1961 . . . married . . .

Island, NY . . . children — 2 . . . age 45.

**Lieutenant
JAMES E. CUTILLO**

assigned to Battalion 33 . . . appointed Lieutenant September 18, 1976 . . . married . . .

. . . children — 2 . . . age 39.

**Firefighter 4th Grade
WILLIAM O'CONNOR**

assigned to Ladder Co. 156 . . . appointed to Department December 15, 1977 . . . married . . .

. . . children — 3 . . . age 29.

**Firefighter 1st Grade
GEORGE S. RICE**

assigned to Ladder Co. 153 . . . appointed to Department August 14, 1965 . . . married . . .

. . . children — 2 . . . age 38.

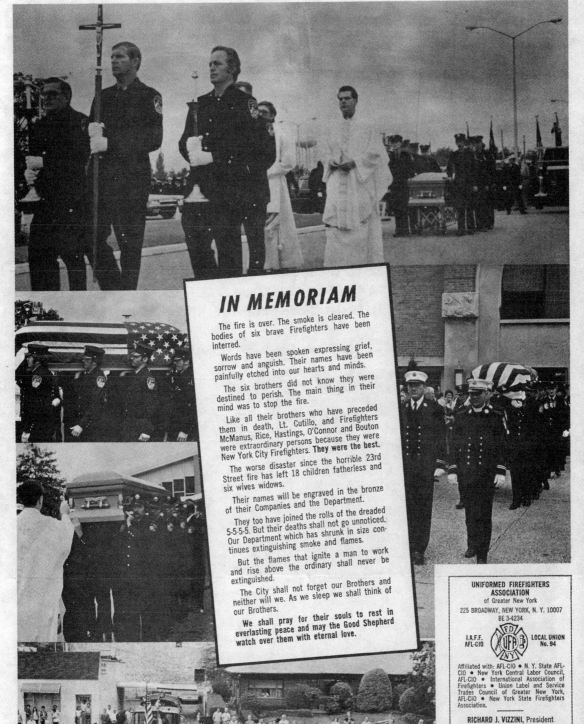

IN MEMORIAM

The fire is over. The smoke is cleared. The bodies of six brave Firefighters have been interred.

Words have been spoken expressing grief, sorrow and anguish. Their names have been painfully etched into our hearts and minds.

The six brothers did not know they were destined to perish. The main thing in their mind was to stop the fire.

Like all their brothers who have preceded them in death, Lt. Cutillo, and Firefighters McManus, Rice, Hastings, O'Connor and Bouton were extraordinary persons because they were New York City Firefighters. **They were the best.**

The worse disaster since the horrible 23rd Street fire has left 18 children fatherless and six wives widows.

Their names will be engraved in the bronze of their Companies and the Department.

They too have joined the rolls of the dreaded 5-5-5-5. But their deaths shall not go unnoticed. Our Department which has shrunk in size continues extinguishing smoke and flames.

But the flames that ignite a man to work and rise above the ordinary shall never be extinguished.

The City shall not forget our Brothers and neither will we. As we sleep we shall think of our Brothers.

We shall pray for their souls to rest in everlasting peace and may the Good Shepherd watch over them with eternal love.

UNIFORMED FIREFIGHTERS ASSOCIATION
of Greater New York
225 BROADWAY, NEW YORK, N. Y. 10007
BE 3-4234

I.A.F.F.
AFL-CIO

LOCAL UNION
No. 94

Affiliated with: AFL-CIO ● N. Y. State AFL-CIO ● New York Central Labor Council, AFL-CIO ● International Association of Firefighters ● Union Label and Service Trades Council of Greater New York, AFL-CIO ● New York State Firefighters Association.

RICHARD J. VIZZINI, President
LOUIS A. SFORZA, Vice-President
ROBERT DiVIRGILIO, Fin. & Rec. Secy.
THOMAS F. REILLY, Treasurer
ROBERT A. LANDAU, Sergeant-at-Arms
NICHOLAS MANCUSO, Chm., Bd. of Trustees
DANIEL L. STROMER, Brooklyn Trustee
PETER D. RICCARDI, Manhattan Trustee
JOHN L. FERRING, Queens Trustee
CARMINE A. DeROSS, JR.,
Staten Island Trustee

* * *

PUBLICITY COMMITTEE
NICHOLAS MANCUSO, L. 44, Chairman
DANIEL L. STROMER, E. 237
PETER D. RICCARDI, L. 6
JOHN L. FERRING, L. 163
CARMINE A. DeROSS, JR. L. 85

Photo courtesy of FDNY

After completion of investigations, a bulldozer
is called in to remove the rubble.

XXXXXXXXXXXXXXXXXXXXXXXXXXXXXXXXXXXXXXXXXXXXXXXXXXXXXXXXXXXXXXXX

From The Bay News, February 12, 1979:

SUPERMART RISES FROM THE ASHES;

PAIN PERSISTS AFTER TRAGIC FIRE

By WILLIAM BACH

On the bitter cold morning of Feb. 6, ten-year-old Chris Fisher was the first customer to walk into the rebuilt Waldbaum's supermarket at 2892 Ocean Ave. Six months earlier six firefighters died in the store when, without warning, the roof of the structure collapsed, dropping them into the burning building.

Due at school two blocks away at 8:30 A.M., young Fisher, pushing an empty shopping cart up and down the aisles, said he woke up especially early for the opening. "I'm not going to buy anything," said the fourth grader, though he paid for some candy before leaving for school. "I heard about the opening two days ago and decided to come down. I don't like that the fire happened but that wouldn't stop me from shopping here."

Two days earlier the mood was austere among the men in the firehouse at 90! Ave. U. In the fire, Ladder Company 153 and Engine Company 254 lost George Rice, a 13-year veteran of the Department and James McManus, who had been a fireman for 17 years. On a calendar hanging in the dispatch booth in the front of the station someone had written over the date of Feb. 2: *Six months since: R.I.P.*

Lieut. Cecil Kent, stationed at Ladder 156, Engine 276 at 1635 E. 16 St., which lost Firemen William O'Connor and Charles Bouton, said some of the men injured in the blaze have sought psychiatric help. He also said one of the widows has been having trouble with one of her children who tells his friends at school that his "daddy is coming home." Other Fire Department sources claimed some of the men injured in the fire have been

pressured to return to active duty and have met resistance from the Department when they asked for psychiatric help, which, they say, the Department has finally provided.

Fireman Charlie Wade, whose father was a fireman, works out of the station on 14th Street. Wade, a 29-year-old firefighter, was first stationed at the firehouse eight months before the Waldbaum's fire. "I will never go to that place," Wade said of the supermarket. "I don't even want to go near it. I drove my girlfriend by the place a few times on the way to Kingsborough College and she said, 'Isn't that where the fire was?' But I just try to shut it out if I go past.

"After the fire I was looking in the back room where there was still some fire. When I came out I saw Tom Higgins, who I thought had gone up to the roof, standing there. I'm not an emotional man, but I picked the guy up and hugged him. Outside of my family it was the first time I knew someone who passed away. I don't even like to think about it, it bothers me so much.

The Heavy Stretcher

"When we were carrying the bodies out we were all just trying to get it done with. You can't afford to be scared on the job. Then we came to one stretcher that was real heavy. I knew right away it was Charlie Bouton. I put my end down and walked outside, went around to the side of the building and wept." Wade's voice choked and he wiped his face as he told the story. "I never cried like that, not since my father died, I mean I just could not stop." Wade shifted uncomfortably while talking and finally turned away.

Blaise Del Bianco, a 25-year-old fireman who works at the 14th Street station, picked up for Wade. "If it changed my opinion about the job, I'd have handed my badge in. A couple of weeks after the supermarket fire I picked someone out of a burning building in a cherry picker and if you save a life once in twenty years on the job you've been a success; our purpose is to save lives.

"The worst part of it for me," Del Bianco said, "was getting the bodies out. There were men I'd spoken to the night before who were so badly burned I could not recognize them. It was the worst experience of my life, but I guess it's a business situation and they have to think of themselves. I think there should be a memorial, though."

"I remember the fire aboard the U.S.S. Constellation when I first started on the Department," said Lieut. Kent. "I wasn't even involved in that fire but I did help carry out the bodies. At one point a charred arm swung out from under a blanket on one of the stretchers and I saw it before one of the men slid it back under. Some of the men joked about the incident in the following weeks, but a few of us, myself included, also had nightmares just from seeing that arm.

"I was at this station for 13 months prior to the Waldbaum's fire and there were never really any fights. You have men living together so there might be disagreements, but it never came to anything at this house. I can tell you that in the weeks after the fire tempers were on edge. Nothing too serious happened, but a few scuffles did break out."

Lower Roof Collapse

Firemen at the blaze, according to various Department officials, went up to the roof under the impression that the fire, said to have started on the mezzanine level, was being contained within the store. The men on the roof had begun cutting ventilation holes in order to allow contained heat and smoke to escape, a usual Fire Department procedure. The men were not aware that the roof they were on was a "rain roof," built over the store's original flat roof to facilitate rain and snow run-off so the roof would not give in during inclement weather. Unknown to the men, the lower, hidden roof was burning and when it gave way the rain roof lost its support and also fell.

"The oddity of this fire," said Lieut. Kent, "is that there was no indication to the men that the roof would fall. Usually a roof gets 'spongy' or soft, or the tar bubbles and we have time to get off. In this case one section went and the whole thing suddenly dropped."

Fire Department Chief Francis Cruthers has filmed a half-hour documentary on the tragic fire, which is being shown periodically on Channel 31 in the New York area. In it, Cruthers outlines the major problems faced by men fighting the fire and discusses what might be done in a similar situation in the future. Displaying sections of the original roof and the rain roof, Cruthers points out that while the original roof suffered extensive fire damage, the rain roof above hardly burned at all.

Additionally, Cruthers says the Department may have inaccurately diagnosed the extent of the fire before sending the men up to the roof, because of the construction under way at the time. Alterations in progress left a whole wall open and Cruthers speculates smoke which escaped through the opening may have caused the Department to underestimate the fire's severity. Cruthers also says initial attempts to put the fire out by people on the scene before calling the Department may have cost his men valuable time.

"On his arrival," Cruthers says on the documentary, "the Chief at the scene followed the professional procedures we follow in the 50,000 fires we fight every year.

"The first line went to the mezzanine and knocked down what fire was visible there. The second line was brought in and so it seemed the fire had been knocked down. So the men were sent up to the roof to ventilate the heat and allow burning objects to escape.

"Because of the rain roof, it wasn't easy to tell where the holes should be cut and so several cuts were made on the top layer. There may not have been adequate communication between those on the roof and in the store, so they may have perceived different fires. As the fire progressed, its severity, location and extent became apparent and just then the roof gave way and 12 men fell in. Officers with years of experience told us they had no indication of the collapse."

Six Survived

Of the 12 who fell through the rain roof six were caught on the second roof and died. Beside Rice, McManus, Bouton and O'Connor, Lieut. James Cutillo, and Harold Hastings perished. The other six men, according to Lieut. Kent, were "lucky." They fell through to the ground and either escaped on their own or were rescued by other firemen.

According to Lieut. Joseph Pavèse at the Fire Department's Medical Division, of the six men who survived the fall through the roof, one man is slated to return to full duty and five others are on light or administrative assignments, currently incapable of returning to firehouse duty.

Captain Rudolph Quatrone of the Fire Department's Investigation Unit said the Brooklyn District Attorney's office is involved in a "criminal investigation" concerning the cause of the fire. Ron Aiello, in charge of the investigation at Brooklyn D.A. Eugene Gold's office, said he could not comment on the investigation.

Waldbaum's spokesmen were reticent on the issue. Waldbaum's Director of Real Estate Aaron Malinsky said, "The Sheepshead community has been a good one for Waldbaum's for a long time. Our stores have had a good response from the area and we are going to continue to serve the community. What happened there was tragic, but because of pending litigation, I'm not free to discuss it." He refused further comment, except to assert that Waldbaum's had not considered turning the property over following the fire.

Sidney Zuckerman, in charge of Waldbaum's advertising said, "I'm not so sure we want any publicity on that store." He refused to answer any further questions. Waldbaum's officials at the store prior to and during the opening refused to comment, saying they didn't want any publicity; *Courier-Life* reporters and photographers were asked to leave the store when they attempted to interview patrons on opening day. Billy Peters, who identified himself as the store's manager, said, "We have nothing to hide but we have our instructions. We don't want any reporters in the store."

Asked to talk about the men they had lived and worked with, words came slowly to the men at the Avenue U station. There was some resistance to sharing their opinions with an outsider; the feeling seemed to be that someone who hasn't experienced what they have in the line of duty might not be able accurately to communicate their emotions. "What I have to say isn't suitable for printing," one said.

(continued)

...Waldbaum's Reopens on Fire Site

Firefighting Isn't Personal

"We can't fight fires on a personal basis," said Lieut. Walter Brett. "You try to do the job. It's more difficult to go out the next time, but it's not like we can say, 'Now we won't fight any more fires at any Waldbaum's,' because if we get the call we will fight fires at Waldbaum's again."

Fireman Di Maria, a ten-year veteran, said. "We remember the fire, but life has to go on. I suppose Waldbaum's has to do what they have to do. Every time we pass there on the truck it stings. Right after it happened things got real quiet here for awhile. I think that any time someone says anything about a supermarket we think of it."

Outside the firehouse on Avenue U hangs a plaque, put up by area business owners. The plaque commemorates the sacrifice made by Rice and McManus. Asked about efforts to have a plaque hung in the Waldbaum's store, Di Maria, standing before the plaque at the firehouse shrugs, "Whatever they do now isn't going to bring them back."

Many of the men were very bitter and, mentioning other Waldbaum's which have burned down in the past two years, speculated on the possibility of arson. "Of course," said one, "you remember the A&P's that burned down a couple of years ago and it just makes you stop and wonder." Others echoed complaints by United Firefighters Association President Richard Vizzini last August, when he said the Department held back on a second alarm until after 9 A.M. to save paying overtime. "They hold 'em back," one fireman said, "Don't let anyone tell you otherwise. They're very cost conscious."

Another fireman said it may not have mattered. "Who knows," he said, "if they had sent out a second alarm earlier we would have had more men there, but who's to say there wouldn't have been more men on the roof as a result. None of this is proven fact."

Lieut. John Donnelly pointed out roofs are opened to save property and that going up on the roofs is something that "has to be done." "We'll still be up there in the future," said Donnelly, "and we have been up there since. We looked at some roofs after this happened, but we have too many other responsibilities to be able to keep up with building methods and architecture."

The ironies surrounding the deaths of the six firemen who perished on a hot August morning rose to the forefront of people's memories last Tuesday when Waldbaum's opened the doors of its new supermarket. On Aug. 2 Harold Hastings was working his last day before a scheduled family vacation to Disney World in Florida. At his home in Hicksville, L.I., the luggage stood packed in the hallway when word of his death came to Mrs. Hastings.

James Cutillo was the lieutenant in charge of the men on the roof. He had been reassigned and need not have gone out on that call.

Charles Bouton and another man at the station decided between themselves earlier in the day which one would go out to another station on a detail and which would stay in the house on 14th Street. Bouton stayed.

Not all of the stories were tragic. Tom Higgins, who was awarded a citation for rescuing men who fell through to the ground, should himself have been on the roof. He was the last one around to the ladder on the roof detail and a lieutenant told him not to go up, to break venetian blinds and glass away from the front windows instead.

The widows of the firemen did not need the store's reopening to remind them of the tragedy.

All Family Men

All of the felled firemen were family men. Kathy Bouton is now raising five children on her own, in Farmingville L.I. "life goes on," she said over the phone on the day the store opened. A child could be heard crying in the background. "I don't take the opening out on the people who work there. I didn't really expect anything from them. It would have been lovely if they had put a plaque up, but I just didn't expect it. As much as this affected myself and my family, I suppose if they offer good prices, people will shop there."

Mrs. Bouton wanted to express her thanks to residents of the Sheepshead area for letters they sent to her and for help offered. "People have been good to us. Better, I think than to the men and the families of the men who were injured. Some of the men injured have been given a hard time, from what I have heard."

George Rice was the son of a fireman. His wife, Carol Ann, is now rearing their two children in Islip Terrace, L.I. Mrs. Rice and other wives picketed in front of the store as it was being rebuilt, hoping to convince Waldbaum's not to reopen. When Waldbaum's ignored petitions collected in the neighborhood, friends and supporters asked Waldbaum's to contact Mrs. Rice about the possibility of hanging a plaque in the store. She was too proud to contact the store herself.

Mrs. Rice pointed out that the Waldbaum's fire has been recognized as the second greatest fire tragedy in the city's history. "If this is the second greatest tragedy, why are the men being forgotten? I still can't forget. It's a lasting scar.

"It's very heartbreaking. They were trying to save the store, no lives were at stake. If lives were saved I'd have said, 'Thank God,' but with six men dead and so many injured, for this store to just open up as though nothing happened is a damn shame."

FIRE: A War That Never Ends

XXXXXXXXXXXXXXXXXXXXXXXXXXXXXXXXXXXXXXXXXXXXXXXXXXXXXXXXXXXXXXXXXXXX

From The New York Daily News, May 23, 1979:

ALL ABOUT BROOKLYN

That day — just the tragedy's beginning

By JOHN HAMILL

ONE DAY last August, the district attorney says, $1,500 changed hands, a gas can and a match were carried into a Brooklyn supermarket and two hours later there were six new widows and 18 fatherless children. And in Brooklyn the people who were left behind will tell you now that "that day," in some ways, was only the beginning of the tragedy.

"Get the rolls, Phil" James McManus shouted to fellow fireman Phil Ruvolo that day, as Company 153 wheeled out of quarters on Ave. U.

"You're going out!" Ruvolo yelled back. "You pick them up on the way back."

McManus, of course, did not come back. He was one of six firemen sucked into a final inferno when the domed roof of Waldbaum's supermarket at 2892 Ocean Ave. collapsed under an arsonist's torch.

Ruvolo, a leather-faced veteran of 22 years and 1,000 fires, was in the second floor TV room of the firehouse on Monday when he heard an arson arrest had been made in the fire that had cost him five friends and nephew William O'Connor that day.

He was asked if firemen made a distinction between death and murder."

"We really haven't had time to sit on it yet," he said.

3 suspected of setting fire

He was told that the district attorney said that three young men from the desolate ghettos of Coney Island were suspected of setting the blaze. Ruvolo, twitching, breathed out and said.

"Terrible. Father, forgive them for they know not what they do," then, pausing. "I guess you could say now that Billy was killed in a fire. Before we just said he died in a fire."

Sitting in a battered armchair, Ruvolo spoke as a soundless hockey game was being played on the color TV behind him. All around were signs of construction.

"They're getting the place ready for a dedication of the plaque to the guys," Ruvolo said. "They've fixed the plumbing and they're even painting the place. It's a hell of a way to get the place fixed up,"

Swallowing, Ruvolo then tried to explain about what happens when death comes to family.

"We're all firemen in this family just about. Me, Billy, his father, his grandfather and now my son Phil. We all live and work in Brooklyn. It's like you're born to this job."

Slowly, in fragments, Ruvolo talked about that day.

The fearful word — collapse

"We could see the smoke from the firehouse. It turned white and that's usually a sign that the fire is knocked down. Then came the magic word. Collapse."

Ruvolo and the rest of the company, which had just reported to work, sped to the fire in their own cars. Crowds had gathered when they arrived and firemen were working with frenzied desperation. One look at the smoking hole told Ruvolo that no one would come out of it alive.

"Heat was knocking people back across the street," Ruvolo said. Across the street, that day, Louise O'Connor was crying with her three children. Billy's wife had come to the firehouse to pick him up and followed the engine to the fire. O'Connor had spotted her from the roof and waved what was a final goodbye. His body was the first that Ruvolo saw being carried out of Aisle 2 of Waldbaums.

"That was it for me, I called it a day right there," Ruvolo remembered.

For Louise, after the reporters had gone, and the mayor had praised the bravery of firemen, and the pensions had been paid, there was only family and Brooklyn to fall back on. She stayed in the apartment two blocks from where she had been raised. Her children stayed in Holy Name school. Where she lives, in Windsor Terrace, people understand about the worth of firemen and getting on with it.

Glad she didn't move

"Call it a premonition or whatever you want," Louise said yesterday. "But before Billy got killed we were looking for a house in Marine Park. Every time we looked I cried. I wasn't ready to leave the neighborhood. Now I'm glad I didn't move. If I was stuck in some suburb I'd be crazy."

Across from her house which faces Prospect Park, children were playing ball, breaking glass and shouting in the spring morning. Two miles away the district attorney and the reporters were discussing six murders. She then explained that her tragedy is also measured in fragments.

"Every day those kids of mine call for their father at least once, usually at night. I'm just glad my family is around the corner. Little things get me these days."

She remembered that a month after that day when her husband died little Billy, her son, asked her what color fire was.

"I told him it was red and orange and yellow."

After she told him that, the six-year-old disappeared into his room and came back a half hour later with a drawing.

"It was a picture of his father falling into the fire."

Jean-Marie's drawing

A few weeks later in the pre-school class that Louise teaches, the children were told to draw a happy picture. Her daughter, Jean-Marie, came forward with a drawing of a store and a black door. Louise asked her what it was.

"That's the store. And that's the door I wished Daddy came out of." The phone was silent for a moment as Louise O'Connor told the story, and then went on.

"That's what arsonists do to children."

Three weeks ago the Ruvolos and the O'Connors held a family reunion at the Sheepshead Bay Yacht Club. There was shrimp and strong drink and a disc jockey spinning tunes. No one spoke of that day, Aug. 2, 1978.

"I asked Louise to dance and she said sure," Ruvolo remembered. We were dancing and all of a sudden she was crying. The guy was playing their wedding song." He paused. "All I could think of was that she was here and not out in Rockland County or some out-of-the-way place."

Ruvolo was asked if he remembered the name of the song.

"Oh sure," he said. "It was called 'We've Only Just Begun.' "

XXXXXXXXXXXXXXXXXXXXXXXXXXXXXXXXXXXXXXXXXXXXXXXXXXXXXXXXXXXXXXXXXXXX

XX

From The New York Daily News, August 2, 1984:

Remember their own
Firemen honor 6 killed at supermart

By VINCENT LEE and JARED McCALLISTER

More than 200 persons, including about 100 off-duty firefighters and Fire Department brass, jammed a Brooklyn church yesterday for a memorial Mass honoring the six firefighters killed in the 1978 Waldbaum's supermarket fire.

The overflow crowd at St. Brendan Church, including Fire Commissioner Joseph Spinnato and department Chief John O'Rourke, heard a sermon of remembrance from the Rev. Thomas Brady, the department's chaplain.

"In the past six years, we have not forgotten," Brady said. "We are here again to offer a Mass of thanksgiving for their lives. We are here because these brave men gave their lives six years ago."

Lt. James Cutillo and firefighters William O'Connor, Charles Boutan, George Rice, James McManus and Harold Hastings were killed Aug. 2, 1978, when the roof of the Waldbaum's supermarket at 2892 Ocean Ave. collapsed as they battled a fierce arson blaze.

IN DECEMBER 1980, Eric Jackson of Brooklyn, then 23, was convicted of six counts of murder and one count of arson in connection with the Waldbaum's fire.

After the service, Spinnato told reporters that it was "the nature of the job (for firefighters) to remember" their fallen comrades. "Every time that bell goes off there's a potential for tragedy."

The Rev. Joseph Finnerty, a priest at St. Brendan, said the memorial Mass was held at the church because it is just a few blocks away from the Ladder 153 firehouse, where several of the victims had worked.

Later yesterday afternoon, Spinnato, O'Rourke, the department commanders in the five boroughs and 150 probationary firefighters participated in a wreath-laying ceremony at the Divison of Training facility on Randalls Island.

"We are here today to remember them," Spinnato said as the wreath was laid at the foot of a monument to the dead firemen that was donated by the Waldbaum's Corp. "Firefighters never forget their own."

XXXXXXXXXXXXXXXXXXXXXXXXXXXXXXXXXXXXXXXXXXXXXXXXXXXXXXXXXXXXXXXXXX

New York City Fire Department Medal of Valor

Photo courtesy of Louise O'Connor

XXXXXXXXXXXXXXXXXXXXXXXXXXXXXXXXXXXXXXXXXXXXXXXXXXXXXXXXXXXXXXXXXXXXX

XXXXXXXXXXXXXXXXXXXXXXXXXXXXXXXXXXXXXXXXXXXXXXXXXXXXXXXXXXXXXXXXXXXXXXXXX

"I believe that if you lose your life at a fire,
you get an automatic pass to heaven."

Jerry Murphy
Firefighter, E.254
(Now Lieut.)

PART 5

"FDNY MEMORIAL DAY"

On the upper west side of Manhattan in Riverside Park is the Firemen's Monument, which was erected in 1912. Looking closely at it and its inscription, one can feel the genuine gratitude of the influential people who shaped a great city at the turn of the century. Not merely a plaque, but a massive stone structure artistically carved. On the north side is a sculpture reminiscent of the "Pieta" by Michelangelo, depicting a fallen fireman in the arms of a woman.

Every October, City officials, honored guests and department members of all ranks assemble there to remember those who have lost their lives in the performance of their sworn duties.

XXXXXXXXXXXXXXXXXXXXXXXXXXXXXXXXXXXXXXXXXXXXXXXXXXXXXXXXXXXXXXXXXXXXXXXXX

For the 1970 Memorial Service, I was asked to be a flag bearer in the color guard. While standing in front of the monument, I heard a UFA board member tell someone the news he had just received; "We just lost another one; from Rescue 1."

That morning on the way to Riverside Park via the West Side Highway, we had noticed the smoke of a fire in progress. That was where Fireman 1st Grade Edward A. Tuite fell to his death. He had been on the job only 5 years and 2 months. As we stood there honoring the past year's eight victims, we already had one for next year.

Seven weeks later (12/7/70), Fireman 2nd Grade Timothy J. Gray of Ladder 34 lost his life, not far from the Monument, at Riverside Drive and 153rd St. Both Gray and Tuite perished after completing their assigned duty: roof ventilation.

Just two years before, Gray and I were freezing our buns at the Probationary Firemen's School on Welfare Island (now Roosevelt Island). We didn't know each other personally, because the class was divided into four platoons of fifty. That's right, 200 men in the class. The two prior classes had 250 each. It seems that the City prefers to hire in spurts after long periods of no appointments.

A person from a small town may find it hard to conceive a Fire Department training school with 250 trainees. In 1981, when I was an instructor at the Fire Academy, there were two classes of 300, aptly named "Operation 600." The total personnel of many departments is less than that and New York has been criticized for having "too much" manpower. But consider this; there are fewer than 2500 (on-duty) members protecting more than 7,000,000 people and a large fortune in property values. And, I might add, at a tiny fraction of the City budget. But that's another story!

Although the Memorial Day ceremony is attended by the news media, it is not considered a major event and is barely mentioned on the six o'clock news, if at all. Indeed, Fire Commissioner Beekman, in his 1978 address, denoted a "generally apathetic interest and reaction" to it.

NOTE: As of Memorial Day 1978, 726 firemen lost their lives in service to the City of New York. In addition to the six killed on August 2nd, another member was honored this day; Firefighter Gerard T. Ganley of Engine Company 258 who died 7/13/78.

Five weeks after the 1978 Memorial Day Service, on November 21st, the 727th member would be added to the FDNY honor roll; Lieut. Robert G. Courtenay of Ladder Company 47.

xxxxxxxxxxxxxxxxxxxxxxxxxxxxxxxxxxxxxxxxxxxxxxxxxxxxxxxxxxxxxxxxxxxx

On October 17, 1978, Commissioner Beekman made an especially moving speech, primarily due to the Waldbaums supermarket fire. Appointment to the position of firefighter is not a prerequisite to Fire Commissioner, but because he came up through the ranks, he was able to express himself as both a firefighter and a leader with a discerning overview of the plight of the entire city.

Rather than quote excerpts of the speech, it is presented here as it appeared in *WNYF Magazine.

Memorial Day speeches are not a usual feature of the magazine. **However, in the 4th issue of 1978, Fire Commissioner Beekman's address was presented as follows:

WNYF (With New York Firefighters) is a quarterly publication by and for members of the Department. Subscriptions and many back issues are available to the public. (See Appendix)

**(c) With permission of NYC Fire Department*

Memorial Day Services Address

BY
COMMISSIONER
AUGUSTUS A. BEEKMAN

Editor's Note: This past October 17th, as in the past forty-nine years, the New York City Fire Department held its annual Memorial Day Services at the site of the Firemen's Monument at Riverside Drive and 100th Street in Manhattan.

Ordinarily a solemn occasion, this year's Memorial Services seemed, if possible, doubly so. The unforeseen and tragic loss of six of our brother firefighters was simply overwhelming. It was a blow that emotionally staggered not only the men of this Department, but all the people of this great City. However, anyone familiar with Fire Department history knows only too well that we have lived with tragedy for over a hundred years. We have, literally, raised ourselves from the ashes, time and time again, to continue the fight "in a war that never ends."

As is customary, many dignitaries attend these Services to address both the members of this Department and the general public; expressing their sincere and heartfelt sympathy for our great and terrible losses. Speaking on behalf of the New York City Fire Department was Fire Commissioner Augustus A. Beekman. As a brother firefighter, he spoke with a clear understanding of a firefighter's hopes, his dreams, his joys, his sorrows, and his fears; and he spoke with a deep knowledge, if you will, of "where a firefighter is coming from."

The staff of W.N.Y.F. is pleased to present that address in its entirety.

"The Fire Department sponsors two major ceremonies each year—the Medal Day ceremony in June where the focus is on life, and the Memorial Day service where the focus is on death. If you've been coming to this ceremony for any number of years, you are aware of the generally apathetic interest and reaction it inspires. This year, as a result of the lingering reaction to the supermarket tragedy on August 2nd, there is a heightened interest in the ceremony and its purpose.

"The days and weeks immediately following August 2nd, produced hundreds of letters of support for the hero firefighters and their families. But, while the community spoke with a voice of support for the families, it, at the same time, spoke to the Fire Department with a questioning voice, and to some extent a voice of admonition. The points at issue are whether or not the Fire Department's approach to its responsibilities is outmoded; does it have a clear perception of the difference between life and property; is it aware that property can be replaced, and that lives should not be endangered in an effort to protect it.

"So, as we meet here this morning in an atmosphere less charged with emotion than that of August 2nd, it is perhaps a good time to speak about life and death, about property and the City of New York, and about the Fire Department's experience and responsibility in all of these areas.

"When we listen to the voice of the community, it is well to recognize that the community speaks with more than one voice; that it speaks with different voices at different times; that it frequently speaks with an emotional voice; and that it sometimes goes speechless.

"Six months before the August 2nd fire, there was another four-alarm fire in Brooklyn on Pine Street in East New York. That fire destroyed or damaged thirteen of a row of fifteen frame private dwellings. If you listened to the voice of the community in the hours and days after the fire, it was not saying these homes are only property and they can be replaced. On the contrary, the community was asking why did my home have to burn? Why could you not stop it from burning? This house represents my life's work and constitutes my life savings.

"Those frame dwellings in East New York are representative of the thousands of frame private dwellings that are found in every Borough, except Manhattan where frames are not allowed. On the average of 3,500 times a year you respond to fires in such dwellings and the concern is always the same. Protect this house; it constitutes my life's work, and represents my life savings.

"If you work in the South Bronx, Harlem, the lower East Side, Williamsburg, South Brooklyn, Bushwick, Bed-Sty, Brownsville, East New York, South Jamaica, Corona—neighborhoods which suffer high fire incidence, but where many do not own their homes, you can't count the number of times you've taken up from a fire leaving the affected families huddled in the street awaiting relocation by the Red Cross. And you've avoided looking into their faces as they despaired over the fact that what little they possessed in life had been destroyed by the fire, and the prospect of starting life anew from a welfare hotel was hardly worth the effort.

"In both the homeowner and rental neighborhoods, you've responded to fires in the small commercial establishments known as "mom and pop" stores—

grocery, candy stores, hardware stores, luncheonettes, and the like. As the fire came under control, you've watched the proprietors approach the chief in a hesitant manner requesting that they be allowed to check the cash register and survey the premises for anything of value. In the course of this effort, you have frequently heard the comment, 'I'm uninsured (or under insured) and my life's work has gone up in this fire.'

"Each year fire fatalities include a few cases wherein the victim had actually escaped the fire in the early stages, but then returned to recover something whose value to the owner was worth the risk, even though the penalty for failure was death.

"These are just a small number of examples to exemplify the fact that the line of demarcation between life and property, which is so clearly defined to those who assess the fire safety effort infrequently and superficially, is less clearly defined to the victims of fire and those who are charged with protecting them.

"The Fire Department's protecting responsibilities can be assessed in a broader context than that of the individual examples that I've just cited. We're now in the World Series period and last year, because of the proximity of a 5 alarm fire to Yankee Stadium, the entire country was treated to a view of the Bronx, burning on wide-screen television and in living color. This was shortly after President Carter had made his shocking discovery that the South Bronx was pretty much of a burned-out wasteland. If you read the reams of type and listened to the numerous media commentators, one could have assumed that the burning of the Bronx was a recent phenomenon—something that had occurred during the past five years.

"But we know that the Bronx has been methodically and systematically burning for at least 15 years—dating back to the early 1960's. And we know, further, that it was preceded by a similar burning experience in Brownsville and parts of East New York. If you listened for the community's voice during the first ten years of this burning experience, what you heard was the sound of silence . . . from government, business, industry, the media, even from the communities which were being decimated by fire.

"In 1968 when Brownsville was at the height of its notoriety, as the most fire ravaged community in America, I spoke to leaders of the Brownsville community council—then the primary voice of Brownsville. I was informed that on a descending scale of 1 to 10—the fire problem in Brownsville would rate about *nine;* after problems like crime, health, education, welfare, sanitation, and employment.

"And if we leave Brownsville and return to the Bronx for a minute, we can make an interesting observation as to the relative effects of crime and fire on a community. For several years, the 41st Precinct in the Bronx was cited as the epitome of an inner city urban police precinct. But in recent years, we've heard much less about Fort Apache. Not because the men of the 41st came up with a sudden and magic formula for crime control, but rather because the area protected by the 41st has been substantially burned out and depopulated. There are fewer people left to commit crime. There are also fewer people left to satisfy the definition and concept of a community. And without communities, you are soon without a city.

"In any case, it was not until a British TV firm produced the documentary, "The Bronx Is Burning," and circulated it here in the States that New Yorkers finally realized that their city was undergoing a 20th Century version of the Burning of Rome. And while

Rome at least had a fiddler, the only music to accompany the burning of Brownsville, or the South Bronx, and more recently of Bushwick, were the fire sirens which pierced the air all hours of the day and night.

"One might well ask what was the Fire Department doing throughout this period. The answer is that it was trying to hold the line with all the resources at its command—with double sections in its Engine Companies and Ladder Companies, and with double and triple sections at the Battalion level. With six-man manning in its Engine Companies, seven-man manning in some of the Ladder Companies, Squads and Rescue Companies. And when this allocation proved to be inadequate, the nightly relocation of fire companies from Manhattan and Queens into the Bronx, and from Queens and sometimes Staten Island and Manhattan into Brooklyn. Overriding this was a containment effort on the part of the firefighters that was so aggressive that the Department finally had to issue written orders telling them to stay out of vacant buildings. Even as it issued the order, the Department knew that most of the buildings weren't fully vacant, but were partially occupied.

"It knew, further, that there is no way to be sure when a vacant building is, in fact, vacant. It knew that vacant buildings are occupied by squatters, by vandals, by junkies, by arsonists. And since the Fire Department does not introduce moral judgment into the performance of its duties, these people were accorded the same protection effort as any other segment of the community.

"Despite this effort, when President Carter stood on Charlotte Street in the Bronx, he found the South and East Bronx pretty well decimated and the North and West Bronx being threatened. When Mayor Koch assumed executive responsibility for the City of New York, he found communities like Bushwick and Washington Heights-Inwood in a state of panic as to the threat of fire to their neighborhoods. We can only speculate as to what the state of the City would be if the Fire Department had accepted the philosophy that if it is only property you need not be so aggressive. The City of New York is surrounded by water and when the burning reached the water's edge, the fires would, no doubt, have burned out. Instead of Mayor Koch worrying about a four million dollar budget, he could borrow $24 from Washington, negotiate a new purchase with the Indians, and we could start the process all over.

"The new prophets of fire fighting strategy tell us, 'it's only property and property can be replaced.' That prophecy hasn't been fulfilled in Brownsville, and as President Carter prepares to allocate $75,000,000.00 to the redevelopment of the Bronx, it will be interesting to see if the redevelopment is as systematic, as dogmatic, and as pervasive as was the destruction.

"The purpose of this somewhat depressing review of the past is to establish the point that the Fire Department is not directed from the perspective of the personal philosophy of the Commissioner and his staff. Rather, its protection responsibilities are defined in the City Charter, and throughout its history the men in the Department have sought to meet those responsibilities through a philosophy of giving a little more rather than a little less. And we would be a little disappointed if this approach is rejected by the community as more than what is expected.

"I said that I would speak about death, meaning fatalities to firefighters. And when a career firefighter speaks of death to an audience composed primarily of

128

firefighters and their families, he does so from a different vantage point than those who have not shared the firefighting experience.

"For me it is permissible to forego the euphemisms through which this subject is usually addressed. In so doing I can state that firefighters do not die as a commitment to duty, nor do they die because laying down one's life is an expectation in the fire service. Dying is not part of the Position Description for any rank in the New York Fire Department. By contrast, the Standards of Performance for every officer rank starts with the responsibility to protect from death or injury those you command. When an Officer delegates duty assignments at the start of a tour, he may assign nozzle men, roof men, forcible entry teams, outside vent men, and the like. But, no one is assigned the responsibility to die. The only time that death becomes a conscious factor in a firefighter's performance, occurs on those occasions when he knowingly and willingly exposes himself to danger in order to save another life. In June, when we honor those acts at the Medal Day ceremony, they are specifically recognized as being above and beyond the call of duty. As such they represent an individual commitment by one human being to another. Such acts are performed by other than firefighters, but firefighters have more opportunities and, fortunately for all concerned, seldom resist such opportunities.

"Firefighters don't die because the Chief Officers who supervise them are unknowledgeable of, or insensitive to, the inherent hazards of firefighting. There is no lateral entry to the Chief Officer ranks of the Fire Department. All men must first serve in the ranks of fireman, lieutenant, and captain prior to becoming a chief. Further, with the exception of the U. S. military, no other profession requires persons working at the supervisory level of our Chief Officers, to share physically the dangers of their subordinates. When the twelve men died at the 23rd Street fire in 1966, the total included two chief officers, one at the Battalion level and one at the Division level. So, the first question asked in the investigation of the August 2nd supermarket fire was for the location of the two Battalion Chiefs who were directing operations. As expected, one was on the roof and the other was in the supermarket where either, or both, could have been victims of the collapse.

"The Chief Officer ranks of the Fire Department are not composed of former kamikaze pilots. They don't, knowingly, place themselves, or the men of their commands, in a position to die.

"As my previous remarks have already suggested, firefighters don't die because the Fire Department has arbitrarily sought to contain fire as aggressively as good judgment will allow, instead of taking the safer option of allowing the fire to burn out. When you're protecting a dense urban environment, you have no other option.

"But men do die, and the reasons are neither unknown or mysterious. Two years ago there was a supermarket collapse on Atlantic Avenue in Brooklyn which resulted in twelve men being thrown into a burning cellar. Fortunately, all but one were recovered safely. However, when the building was examined after the fire, it was found that the substructure consisted of three foundations constructed during the Civil War, whereas the superstructure was constructed after World War II. I cite this to exemplify the structural complexities and uncertainties of a city that is over 300 years old, and one which, despite its brick and stone facade, is conducted of, primarily, wood.

"To construction complexities we can add those of content and occupancy. Contents which reflect the miracles of post World War II and space age technology, but which also present new and undefined dangers to firefighters as exemplified by PVC.

"Then we have the uncertainties of occupancy in an immigrant city which for 300 years has had to assimilate different peoples and different cultures. When Brooklyn firefighters speak of a Bushwick overnight bag, they're not talking about Samsonite luggage. They're talking about a gasoline can whose contents are used by some residents as a form of self-expression. In the Bronx, too, we've had evidence of this form of expression in the tragic social club fire with the loss of 24 lives. When the community speaks with this unfamiliar and unexpected voice, the firefighters are also on the receiving end of the message.

But this mix of structure, occupancy, and content is only a part of the problem. Firefighting is conducted in an environment wherein those defenses which nature has assigned us for self-preservation are substantially impaired; at a time when they are most needed. The sense of sight, of touch, of smell, of hearing, are all rendered less acute during the firefighting effort. And, if we're getting older, as we all must, or if we are fighting the second or third major fire during the course of a tour, one's stamina, agility, judgment, and reflexes are also reduced in efficiency. This, too, is only a part of the problem.

"A common expression in firefighting is, 'move in and kill the fire.' But, fire doesn't roll over and play dead when the firefighters arrive. Fire is included as one of the Four Horsemen of the Apocalypse because, from the beginning of time, it has defied man's ability to control it. The annual toll of 10,000 persons and 150 firefighters is mute evidence of fire's ability to kill in return. And this, too, is only a part of the problem.

"While we are created in the image and likeness of God, we are, unfortunately, not blessed with His perfection or His infallibility. Here in New York we perform at about a 95% level in the area of life safety. But 5% is a lot of slippage in a profession dealing with life and death. While the goal is to reduce this gap, it nevertheless must be recognized that 100% perfection is not likely to be achieved. And this, too, is only a part of the problem.

"We could spend the remainder of the morning listing factors which are a part of the dangers that are inherent to firefighting.

"In the light of all I've said so far, some might wonder if we're going to leave here this morning in a depressed state, a state of melancholy. We haven't done so in the thirty-two years I've been in this Department, including the years immediately following 23rd Street.

"Firefighting is a profession for optimists; and optimism, bordering on the bravado, controls the work attitude of most of our fire companies. The work attitude not only offsets the generally negative work environment of the professional firefighter, but also causes competence to evolve as a self-fulfilling prophecy. It is an attitude which gives support to those who would romanticize the firefighter in song or poetry.

"As professional firefighters, the poetry with which you can best identify is a poem to which you were exposed in your grammar school years. It was written by the 19th Century British writer Rudyard Kipling, and we can close this talk by paraphrasing its opening line, 'You have to keep your head—even when those about you are losing theirs.' " ▲

Photo courtesy of Herb Eysser

XXXXXXXXXXXXXXXXXXXXXXXXXXXXXXXXXXXXXXXXXXXXXXXXXXXXXXXXXXXXXXXXXXXXXXX

XXX

"DUTY and SACRIFICE"

(Firefighters' motto)

PART 6

"THE FIREMEN'S MONUMENT:
FROM INSPIRATION TO FRUITION"

Upon completion of Part 5, I was not satisfied with it due to lack of a good photograph of the Firemen's Monument, and I was also curious about its historical background. Seeking access to the Fire Department Library, I discovered that all the books were in storage pending a new location.

Well, thanks to Patricia Gonzalez of the FDNY's Publications Unit and Mr. Herb Eysser, Manhattan Dispatcher, I received enough historical data and photos for another book. Here is but a brief outline of how the New York City Firemen's Monument came to be:

XXXXXXXXXXXXXXXXXXXXXXXXXXXXXXXXXXXXXXXXXXXXXXXXXXXXXXXXXXXXX

At a 3-alarm fire in the early morning hours of   February 14, 1908, Deputy Chief Charles W. Kruger lost his life after serving 36 of his 57 years with the Fire Department.   So remarkable was his reputation, that many prominent people agreed that a monument should be erected in his honor. Shortly thereafter, it was decided that the monument should be in honor of all fallen firemen, past and future, regardless of rank.

A newspaper, The New York Globe, immediately started a subscription fund (with a $100 donation) for the memorial and acknowledged every donor by name and amount. A few millionaires coughed up $1000 each and one philanthropic woman gave $5000. But most donations were under $100, many as little as 10 or 25 cents.

The Globe also printed letters from the donors showing the tremendous support for the project. One letter, which obviously touched the hearts of the editors, was reproduced in its handwritten form. (page 138)   The contents of their savings bank was one dollar.

When the fund reached more than $50,000, bids were taken from architects, but the approved design carried an estimate of about $90,000.

After a plea from Isidor Strauss, chairman of the Memorial Fund Committee, to the Mayor and the Board of Estimate and Apportionment, $40,000 was appropriated in November of 1910.

Although erected in 1912, the monument was not unveiled and dedicated until September 5, 1913. In spite of many years of social chaos, both city and worldwide, it remains, peacefully overlooking the Hudson River and welcoming visitors to contemplate the goodness of the human spirit.

To express my gratitude, I shall use this space to state that I am thankful for people like Chief Kruger, who led by example, and thereby inspired others to do likewise. I am thankful for those who respected and loved him, and without whom the Firemen's Monument would not have been built as a tangible recognition of duty and sacrifice.

I'm also thankful that the City of New York, in the face of fiscal constraints, has recently seen fit to refurbish the monument after some weather damage. And finally, I am thankful that I was not called upon to join the ranks of the honor roll.

Following is more historical data behind the NYC Firemen's Monument, courtesy of Herb Eysser:

XXXXXXXXXXXXXXXXXXXXXXXXXXXXXXXXXXXXXXXXXXXXXXXXXXXXXXXXXXXXXXXX

New York Globe Feb 17. 1908

He Never Said "Go," but "Come, Boys."

PROMINENT MEN JOIN IN MOVEMENT TO ERECT MONUMENT TO CHIEF KRUGER, KILLED WHILE ON DUTY

DEPUTY CHIEF C. W. KRUGER
Memorial Shaft to Be a
Tribute to the Man
Who Did Things
and Knew No
Fear.

EVERY ONE IN THE CITY
CAN HELP SUBSCRIPTION

Plans Are to Be Pushed With
the Hope That the Monu-
ment Can Be Unveiled
on Day of the Fire-
men's Parade.

FIREMEN'S MEMORIAL FUND COMMITTEE

The Right Rev. HENRY C. POTTER, Episcopal Bishop for New York, Chairman.

Gen. THOMAS L. JAMES, president of the Lincoln National Bank, Treasurer.

ANDREW CARNEGIE.

HUGH BONNER, Fire Commissioner and former chief of the Department.

GEORGE W. BABB, president of the New York Board of Fire Underwriters.

ISIDOR STRAUS, of R. H. Macy & Co.

HENRY W. TAFT, member of the law firm of Strong & Cadwalader.

THE REV. H. A. BRANN, D. D., Rector of St. Agnes's Church.

EGERTON L. WINTHROP, JR., president of the Board of Education.

CORNELIUS N. BLISS, senior member of Bliss, Fabyan & Co

HAMILTON W. MABIE, editor of The Outlook.

From The New York Globe,

February 19, 1908

XXXXXXXXXXXXXXXXXXXXXXXXXXXXXXXXXXXXXXXXXXX

xxx

Firemans Herald Feb 22 1908.

DEATH OF DEPUTY CHIEF CHARLES W. KRUGER

Deputy Chief Charles W. Kruger of New York died at his post of duty at a fire at 215 and 217 Canal street about 4 A. M. on Friday, February 14. An alarm from Station 147 at 1.03 A. M., followed by two other alarms, was for a fire that destroyed the five-story building at 217 Canal street, occupied as a looking glass frame manufactory, and spread to the top stories of adjoining buildings. The fire started on the third floor and extended to the roof and the subcellar. The sub-cellar and basement was used to store lumber mouldings, loose excelsior, rubbish, etc., and barrels under the sidewalk were filled with shavings. The first floor was the office and salesroom, the second floor stock, third and four floors work rooms, and fifth floor, storage for shellac, wood alcohol, benzine, etc. The loss was about $50,000.

After a several hours hard fight the fire, a most stubborn one, was extinguished except in the lower stories and basement of the building in which it originated. It was difficult to reach the fire in the basement from the front and to gain access to it from the rear or through the wall separating it from the basement of the next building that Chief Kruger was leading his men when he met his death. He entered the basement of 215 through the sidewalk entrance. The basement was empty and dark and the only light was from the lanterns of the chief and other firemen. The basement was filled with smoke. Following behind Chief Kruger was his driver, Andy Horgenrother, and behind him the other firemen, members of Truck 8. The chief, who was some distance in the lead, fell through a hatchway opening into the sub-cellar, which was partially filled with water. He called to his driver to assist him. His driver, who was partially overcome, called to others for assistance. The chief, who was a heavy man, was rescued with some difficulty in an unconscious condition and taken to the sidewalk, where Dr. Henry M. Archer, a department physician, and other physicians from the hospital worked over him for a long time, but it was useless, they were unable to revive him.

Chief Kruger's death is certified to be due to submersion and shock. When he was brought out of the cellar the medical men say that there was no radical pulse and the stethoscope failed to reveal any heart sounds. Oxygen was immediately administered and the strongest and most powerful cardiac and respiratory stimulants were given by inhalation and hypo-

continuously applied for an hour. Newspapers reports say that no oxygen was used, which is untrue. Water was removed from his lungs and an upholstering tack was taken from his mouth. Six other firemen were overcome, and it is believed that it was a deficiency of the proper amount of oxygen in the cellar and not gases or fumes

DEPUTY CHIEF CHARLES W. KRUGER,
New York.

that caused it. The gas had been shut off at commencement of the fire.

The hatchway was about midway the length of the basement on the opposite side from the sidewalk entrance. There were no stairs leading to the subcellar, which is contrary to the law, which is it is claimed that steps were subsequently found on the sub-cellar floor that might have been used for this purpose. Seven years ago a fireman fell through the same hatchway during a fire and was injured. The fire spread to the next building, the Barry Howard house, named in honor of Barry Howard, who was chief of the volunteer department from 1857 to 1860.

The funeral of Chief Kruger was held on Sunday, Feb. 16, a magnificent day, and was one of the largest and most impressive ever held in this city. The sidewalks along the route from the house to where the firemen and others left the procession in the upper part of the city were thronged with people, and most of the men bared their heads as the hearse passed. The floral offerings filled two large automobile trucks and were

CANAL STREET FIRE, NEW YORK.
Where Deputy Chief C. W. Kruger lost his life.
The x indicates where Chief Kruger entered
the basement of No. 215.

from many people and organizations, including a large cross from the Baltimore Fire Department. Over 500 firemen in uniform in command of Chief Croker and Deputy Chief William Duane, with divisions in charge of Battalion Chief G. L. Ross and P. H. Short, acted as escort. Fire Commissioner Hugh Bonner and his son were next behind the hearse. The pall bearers were Battalion Chiefs C. H. Shay, J. F. King and J. F. Kane of Manhattan; Henry Hauck, of Brooklyn; W. E. Lawrence, of Rockaway, and Thomas Larkin, of Jamaica. Andy Horgenrother, Chief Kruger's driver for many years, walked in the rear. Many prominent citizens and city

officials were present, including former Fire Commissioners Sturgis, Hayes, O'Brien and Lantry, and many former officers and privates of the department. The Ripsaw Club of which the chief was a member, was also in the procession. The police band furnished the music. There were fifty carriages. On the casket was Chief Kruger's fire hat and a wreath of white carnations from Mayor McClellan, the city's contribution.

A short service was held at his late home, No. 226 East Fifty-eighth street, at 1 o'clock. The principal service was held at the St. Thomas Episcopal Church at Fifth avenue and Fifty-third street. Bishop Henry C. Potter preached the sermon, assisted by Rev. E. M. Stires, rector of the St. Thomas Church, and Rev. E. H. M. Knapp, one of the fire department chaplains. The music was furnished by Manager Conreid of the Metropolitan Opera House, who requested the privilege. This was the first time Bishop Potter ever officiated at the funeral of a fireman. In part he said:

"No more tragic event has occurred in the history of this metropolis and in fact in the history of the fire department in any community of this country than the one which resulted in the death of the commanding officer whom we are here to-day gathered to honor. In fact, during the past few weeks there has been a series of tragic events happening among that most admirable body of men, and it would be extremely ungrateful if we failed to allow such a series of losses of life in the performance of their hazardous work to pass without comment. Has it ever occurred to you that the heroism and self-sacrifice on the part of these men is incontrovertibly finer than was ever displayed in any battle field of old? We are here to-day to pay tribute to one of these modern self sacrificing heroes to whom we are all indebted. And in this particular case if I were to erect a monument and carve in the stone words to commemorate his memory, I would use the words: "He never said 'Go,' but 'Come, boys.'"

As the cortege passed the station of Engine Co. No. 23 in Fifty-eighth street the company was lined up and saluted, and the muffled bell tolled at intervals until the last carriage went by. Interment was at Woodlawn Cemetery, where many firemen and citizens of Yonkers awaited the arrival of the procession at nightfall. Many flags throughout the city were at half mast.

Deputy Chief Charles Washington Kruger, who was one of the ablest and most beloved members ever in the New York Fire Department, was born in this city 57 years ago. He was educated in the public

XX

schools and was a machinist by trade. On July 3. 1872, he entered the department as an assistant engineer of a steam fire engine. On September 27 he was promoted to assistant foreman and held that position for eighteen years, but most of that time he was acting foreman of Truck Co. No. 10, located in Fulton street, then one of the most important truck companies in the department, which covered all the lower section of the city. On January 1, 1895, he was promoted to foreman, on April 1, 1897, to chief of battalion, and on April 1, 1903, to deputy chief. From Dec. 1, 1903, when Chief C. D. Purroy resigned, until Feb. 9, 1904, when Chief E. F. Croker was reinstated, Deputy Chief Kruger was in command of the department. He sent the apparatus that went to the Baltimore conflagration on Feb. 9, 1904. He was always located in the downtown sections, the most hazardous of the city. As battalion chief he had charge of the first battalion, which includes all of that section below the City Hall, and as deputy chief he had charge of all the district below Fourteenth street until a year or so ago, when his district was divided and a new division created in the lower section of the city. His district was renumbered and is now Division 2, with headquarters in Lafayette street, a short distance from Canal street. Some of the largest and best handled fires were under his management. His record as a fireman and commander is without a blemish and unexcelled. He met with numerous narrow escapes and was always a leader and always looking after the safety of his men. No fireman ever feared to go where he ordered them to go. They had the most implicit confidence in him and would follow him anywhere. When a captain he won a Stevenson medal for having the best disciplined company in the department. He was selected by Chief Bonner for chief of the Springfield, Mass., department when a change was made in that city in 1894, but declined the position when he learned of conditions that existed in that department.

He is survived by a widow, a daughter of fifteen and two sons, aged six and eight, by his first wife, who died a few years ago. He was married the second time about one year ago. His home was at Arverne in the Rockaway Beach section of the city. He recently purchased a small farm at Freeport. L. I., and was contemplating an early retirement from the department. to pass the remainder of his days on this farm.

In general orders Commissioner Bonner announced Chief Kruger's death to the department as follows:

"With sincere regret it becomes my painful duty to announce to the department the death of Deputy Chief Charles W. Kruger while in the discharge of his duty at fire at 215 Canal street on February 14, 1908. We all admired the chief for his sterling qualities as a man, his ability and skill as a fireman having long since been conceded. A graduate from the old school of firemen, he possessed the rare gift on sight of danger to locate the department forces so effectually in the line of attack as to almost invariably terminate with success and honor to his professional skill as a chief.

"We humbly bow to the will of the inevitable which has deprived the department and the city of the services of this noble chief. It remains only for the members of the department to pay tribute to the memory of our honored dead."

Chief Croker in his order to the department said:

"The Fire Department of the city has suffered a great loss; he was at all times to be relied upon. Of undoubted courage and possessing magnificent personal qualities, he commanded the respect and admiration not only of his superior officers but of men of all ranks and grades with whom he came in contact. Appointed in 1872, through devotion and fidelity to duty his merit won for him deserving promotion until he became deputy chief and on many occasions commanded the department in the absence of the chief. His entire life and record was a splendid example to follow, and the heartfelt sympathy of the entire department goes out to his widow and family in the great loss they have sustained."

Nearly all the daily newspapers contained editorials eulogizing the dead chief, and never has the city mourned the death of one of its faithful servants more sincerely than it now mourns the death of Deputy Chief Charles W. Kruger.

From The Firemens Herald,

February 22, 1908

XXXXXXXXXXXXXXXXXXXXXXXXXXXXXXXXXXXX

Globe February 21 1908

313 E 43 St

Feb 20th/1908

The Globe

5 Dey St City

Please except the contents of our saving bank to help a Monument in Memmory of our dear papa John J McConnell who lost his life in the Worth St fire on Feb 4th Hoping all other firemen Children will help

Yours Truly

Teresa McConnell
Julia McConnell
George McConnell
Elizabeth McConnell

FUND FOR THE KRUGER AND FIREMEN'S MEMORIAL

J. P. Morgan	$100.00
Joe Gans	100.00
Wyckoff, Church & Partridge	15.00
Lambert Bros.	10.00
George H. Downing	2.00
A. E. Bastedo, Hastings, N. Y.	2.00
Hugh H. Blair	1.00
Teresa McConnell	.25
Julia McConnell	.25
George McConnell	.25
Elizabeth McConnell	.25
T. L. Morison	.10
Patrick J. Kilian	.10
Erwin Kahn	1.00
Saul Tasman	.10
D. J. Burtis	1.00
Henry Kletzer	1.00
Ami	1.00
Frugone, Balletto & Pellegatte Co.	10.00
From Counter Banks	9.98
Previously acknowledged	608.60
Total	$863.88

NOTE: The above handwritten letter is from the children of Fireman John J. McConnell of Engine Company 4, who died in the line of duty on February 4, 1908.

XXXXXXXXXXXXXXXXXXXXXXXXXXXXXXXXXXXXXXXXXXXXXXXXXXXXXXXXXXXXXXXXX

xxx

South side sculpture symbolizing "Duty"

North side sculpture symbolizing "Sacrifice"

xxxxxxxxxxxxxxxxxxxxxxxxxxxxxxxxxxxxxxxxxxxxxxxxxxxxxxxxxxxxxxxxxxxxx

Firemen's Monument at 100th St. and Riverside Drive.

East side (rear) with inscription

Photo courtesy of FDNY

XXXXXXXXXXXXXXXXXXXXXXXXXXXXXXXXXXXXXXXXXXXXXXXXXXXXXXXXXXXXXXXXX

xxxxxxxxxxxxxxxxxxxxxxxxxxxxxxxxxxxxxxxxxxxxxxxxxxxxxxxxxxxxxxxxxxxxx

ON THE FIREMEN'S MONUMENT INSCRIBED IN STONE
ARE THESE WORDS:

* * * * * *

TO THE MEN OF THE FIRE DEPARTMENT

OF THE CITY OF NEW YORK

WHO DIED AT THE CALL OF DUTY

SOLDIERS IN A WAR THAT NEVER ENDS

THIS MEMORIAL IS DEDICATED

BY THE PEOPLE OF OF A GRATEFUL CITY

* * * * * *

xxxxxxxxxxxxxxxxxxxxxxxxxxxxxxxxxxxxxxxxxxxxxxxxxxxxxxxxxxxxxxxxxxxxx

Shortly after the Memorial Fund Committee was formed, Fire Commissioner Hugh Bonner, a committee member, died of pneumonia and other complications. Elected to replace him was Edward F. Croker, Chief of the Department from 1899 to 1911.

EDWARD F. CROKER
(1899-1911)

Self-described as a persistent agitator for the erection of the monument, Chief Croker is perhaps best known for the following statement of principles which is often called the "Firemen's Creed." It is quoted often because it embodies the true spirit of a dedicated firefighter of the past, present and future.

Photo courtesy of FDNY

XXXXXXXXXXXXXXXXXXXXXXXXXXXXXXXXXXXXXXXXXXXXXXXXXXXXXXXXXXXXXX

"I have no ambition in this world but one, and that is to be a fireman. The position may, in the eyes of some, appear to be a lowly one; but, we who know the work which the fireman has to do, believe that his is a noble calling. There is an adage which says that, "Nothing can be destroyed, except by fire!" We strive to preserve from destruction the wealth of the world, which is the product of the industry of men, necessary for the comfort of both the rich and the poor. We are defenders from fires of the art which has beautified the world; the product of the genius of men and the means of refinement of mankind. But, above all, our proudest endeavor is to save lives of men the work of God Himself. Under the impulse of such thoughts, the nobility of the occupation thrills us and stimulates us to the deeds of daring, even at the supreme sacrifice. Such considerations may not strike the average mind, but they are sufficient to fill to the limit our ambition in life and to make us serve the general purpose of human society."

Chief Edward F. Croker
New York City Fire Department

XXXXXXXXXXXXXXXXXXXXXXXXXXXXXXXXXXXXXXXXXXXXXXXXXXXXXXXXXXXXXXXX

Common Signs and Symptoms of a Psychologic Reaction to a Catastrophic Event

Emotional	Cognitive	Behavioral
Anticipatory anxiety	Blaming someone	Change in activity
Denial	Confusion	Change in speech
Generalized anxiety	Poor attention span	Withdrawal
Panic reactions	Difficulties with decision	Angry outbursts
Shock	making	Suspiciousness
Fear	Heightened or lowered	Change in communications
Survivor guilt	alertness	Change in interactions with
Uncertainty	Increased or decreased	others
Intensified emotional	awareness of surroundings	Increase or decrease in
reactions	Increased vigilance	food consumption
Depression		Increase in alcohol
Grief		consumption
Inappropriate emotions		Disrupted sleep
		Intensified fatigue
		Antisocial acts
		More frequent visits to
		physicians for
		nonspecific complaints
		Overactive vigilance to
		environment
		Changes in overall health

XXX

"Who will save the saviors?"

PART 7

"THE CASE FOR CISD"

On September 30, 1986, I attended a lecture on Critical Incident Stress De-Briefing [CISD] given by Jeffrey T. Mitchell, Ph.D.; a former paramedic and volunteer firefighter with more than a few stories of traumatic experience.

I learned a lot during that lecture. I learned that it's normal to feel many different emotions after a tragic incident that you were supposed to resolve, but couldn't. I learned that there is a "rescue personality" which comprises similar traits among rescue workers. In summary, I learned that there was an "available program" to help alleviate the trauma of critical incident stress.

XXXXXXXXXXXXXXXXXXXXXXXXXXXXXXXXXXXXXXXXXXXXXXXXXXXXXXXXXXXXX

The lecture was held at the Fire Academy, so I knew that then-Fire Commissioner Spinnato was aware of its content. Nevertheless, I wrote to him to express my support for a CISD program for FDNY, because I knew that many members might have been helped after the Waldbaums fire, if such a program was available.

My letter was not acknowledged, so I presumed that due to voluminous mail it wasn't practical to acknowledge every piece of correspondence. About 18 months later, while detailed to headquarters, I followed up on that letter and learned that there was no record of its receipt. Was the Department considering a CISD program? By all indications, it was not.

Around mid-1988, I thought I had a brainstorm. If I could get the Chief Medical Officer of FDNY's Bureau of Health Services, Dr. Cyril Jones, to agree there is a need for a CISD program, then he could recommend it to the Commissioner with more weight than a lowly lieutenant.

Part of my brainstorm was to attempt informal contact with Dr. Jones and avoid getting lost in a paper shuffle through normal channels.

XXXXXXXXXXXXXXXXXXXXXXXXXXXXXXXXXXXXXXXXXXXXXXXXXXXXXXXXXXXXX

I had a friend detailed to the Bureau of Health Services, who became my "entrance through the back door." He described Dr. Jones as a fine gentleman with a genuine concern for the members; an opinion with which I heartily concurred and presumed.

After relaying some papers I had put together (mostly articles written by Dr. Mitchell), my friend informed me that Dr. Jones had already been working on a program to be adapted to the needs of FDNY. Finally, in the latter part of 1989, then-Commissioner Bruno announced the forming of the "FDNY Crisis Response Team." The logistics of the program are some-what sketchy, but the important thing is that the need has been acknowledged.

So, what was my part in getting FDNY to provide psycho-logical support for members involved in critical incident stress? The answer is, "Absolutely nothing!" It would have happened anyway. It was too essential not to have happened.

Three months after the Waldbaums fire (11/78), the New York Post followed up on eight firemen who were still out on medical leave. Following are three articles by reporter Patrick Sullivan and a New York Post editorial statement:

XXXXXXXXXXXXXXXXXXXXXXXXXXXXXXXXXXXXXXXXXXXXXXXXXXXXXXXXXXXXXX

BROOKLYN FIRE HEROES SEND S.O.S. TO CITY

POST EXCLUSIVE by PATRICK W. SULLIVAN

Firemen who survived a blazing roof collapse where six others died said yesterday that their lives have been nightmares ever since and complained that the Fire Dept. is ignoring their pleas for medical treatment.

They say the experience of seeing and hearing six of their comrades die in a sea of flames on Brooklyn's Ocean Avenue last Aug. 2 has shattered their lives and left them with permanent pyschological scars.

"The day of the accident you are treated like a hero and after that you are a bag of crap," said fireman Hal Plaut, 30, one of eight surviving firefighters on the roof inteviewed by the Post.

"Only one of the eight wants to go back to fire duty. The others say the psychological scars make it impossible.

And all are furious with the Fire Dept.'s medical treatment since the blazing inferno and sent an S.O.S. to the city through The Post.

All had suffered serious injuries and all have had varying degrees of emotional problems which have had serious effects on their family life.

Most were forced to go to private doctors, and those who could afford it have gone to their own psychiatrists.

"That these men should be denied any phase of medical care is a shocking state of affairs," said their lawyer, Harry H. Lipsig.

The nightmares of the fire are different for each man.

For Hal Plaut, there are the dreams that "I'm burn

The New York you never see

PAGE 15

---

ing, my house is burning. I have installed smoke detectors everywhere. Often in the middle of the night, I wake up and check the stove."

Donald King, 46, keeps seeing and hearing the firemen trapped with him in the cockloft. He went into a panic recently when his car stopped for a moment inside a car wash.

"Occasionally," recounts William Kelly, the 44-year-old father of four, "I wake up believing the floor is going out from under me."

For John Madigan its the screams — "I hear them because I know there were screams, I screamed. I wake up screaming."

Lipsig, their lawyer, says

Continued on Page 7

that the most glaring example of the men's problems was the two months Madigan kept telling the Fire Dept. doctors of his chest pains.

Madigan finally went to a heart doctor who put him in the hospital that afternoon. His heart sac was full of blood and because of the delay it could not be taken out with a needle and they had to cut him open.

"They told me I should not have even walked into the hospital," Madigan said. "And you know the Wednesday before the medical department put me on continued light duty and said there was nothing wrong with my heart."

"He was almost going into shock," said the surgeon Dr. Emile A. Naclerio, adding that Madigan's problem was definitely a result of his fall and that he is now close to becoming a "cronic invalid."

The department's steadfast refusal to pay for pyschological therapy — even after an official psychiatrist recommended it for some — also has the firefighters upset.

Kelly was given authorization for intensive therapy after the nightmares kept him up and he called in sick from exhaustion and anxiety. But the balding, soft-spoken man who had never "gone sick" in 18 years as a firefighter saw the authorization inexplicably quashed by the Medical Dept. administrator.

Plaut will not drive a car because the other day he became so enraged when cut off that he jumped out and punched the driver.

"They keep giving me a month's medical leave, what am I supposed to do, cure myself?" he asked. "I go down there and they totally discount pyschological trama. It is very frustrating."

Although his wife has just undergone a serious operation, the handsome father of one is paying $60 an hour to see a psychiatrist.

Even though 80 per cent of Plaut's face was burned, he was sent home after the fire. "I kept saying to my wife, 'Am I really hurt or what?' I finally went to the burn center and they wanted to know what the hell I was doing walking around."

Deputy Fire Commissioner John Mulligan, when told about the men's complaints, said he had personally visited the injured men at five hospitals in the hours after the fire to see that everything possible was being done for them.

Mulligan promised to look into the current medical efforts being made for the men, but said he would have no comment about the charges until he had done so.

Meanwhile, the eight men try to cope the best they can.

XXX

Wife tells of fireman hero's nightmare life

Post Exclusive
By PATRICK SULLIVAN

The worst frustration for Mary Campbell has been being powerless to do anything about the nightmares and anxiety her fireman husband has suffered since his escape from the tragic Brooklyn fire where six of his colleagues died 109 days ago.

Also frustrating has been the inability to get the Fire Dept. to provide the psychiatric help she feels her husband needs.

The mother of six desperately wants the help because life at home has been totally disrupted since Aug. 2 when her husband Terrance was hurled into a sea of flames as the roof under him collapsed. Somehow the 20-year veteran crawled out, his hair, coat and legs burning furiously.

'TRYING TO WAKE HIM'

"It's the waking up in the middle of the night, hearing him having a nightmare, screaming, crying," the 40-year-old housewife explained. "Then trying to wake him up, trying to tell him where he is. Then sitting up talking until the wee hours of the morning and still have to be up bright and early to get everyone on their way."

Yesterday the Sunday edition of The Post reported that seven other men who had to claw through the inferno to safety were experiencing similar nightmares and anxieties and were also unhappy with the Fire Dept.'s refusal to offer psychiatric counseling.

Like some of the others, Campbell has been forced to pay for private therapy.

When 17-year-old Mary Campbell first saw her father in the burn center "he looked like somebody in a concentration camp. He had no hair. His eyes looked so big and they had no expression."

'IT'S BEEN HARD'

Since then the pretty teenager said "its been hard. He's different, little things really annoy him."

When 4-year-old Teresa first saw her father come in the house, his ears black, his head bald, "she wouldn't go near him," Mrs. Campbell said. "She absolutely refused to be alone with him. It was a full month before she would sit on his lap."

The badly burned ears also became a family problem.

Campbell was not allowed to sleep on the ears because if the circulation was cut off, he would lose them. They also bled continuously.

"The kids got flashlights and would get up at night and shine them on me," Campbell said, in his neat two-story Brooklyn home. "They'd say 'Dad, you're sleeping on your ears.'"

The blood forced his wife to change the sheets three times a day.

Gradually Campbell and his wife realized he needed therapy.

"I'm not trained, so I could sit for days on end and talk to him but it would do no good," Mrs. Campbell said. "I am no more capable of treating him psychologically than I was of treating those burns on the day of the fire.

"A lot of my energies were given into trying to get help . . . actually fighting with the Fire Dept."

The medical administrator "gave us a flat 'no'" and jumped the chain of command to Asst. Chief Joseph A. Flynn.

An appointment was arranged but, Mrs. Campbell said, "we were told nothing could be done."

Mrs. Campbell found a nearby clinic and therapy started immediately.

"Terry has been a fireman for almost 20 years," Mrs. Campbell said. "He always did his job. He was a fireman when I married him. The biggest hurt has been the fact that these people didn't believe him."

Because firemen "work as a team," Campbell said he does not think he wants to go to another fire — "I might chicken out on the guys when they need me."

It was a sentiment echoed in yesterday's Post by the other survivors.

From The New York Post, 11/20/78. Reprinted with permission.

XXXXXXXXXXXXXXXXXXXXXXXXXXXXXXXXXXXXXXXXXXXXXXXXXXXXXXXXXXXXXXXXX

149

From The New York Post, 11/21/78. Reprinted with permission:

Koch orders probe of hero firemen's plight

By PATRICK SULLIVAN

Mayor Koch today ordered an investigation into the treatment of firemen who survived the fiery roof collapse last August where six men died.

The survivors have complained about the lack of treatment from the Fire Dept. for the psychological disorders they have suffered since their escape from death at a supermarket blaze in Brooklyn's Sheepshead Bay.

Fire Commissioner August A. Beekman acknowledged Koch's order and said, 'I am looking into this right now and I will report to the Mayor."

It was also learned that City Council President Carol Bellamy recently sent a letter to Beekman after the wife of one fireman, Terrance Campbell, wrote last month about their inability to get the kind of psychological treatment they wanted.

The letter recommended that "in light of these particularly tragic circumstances, I would urge that the Dept. give every consideration to fireman Campbell's request" for further assistance.

Campbell and seven other firefighters have told The Post of suffering recurring nightmares, depression and anxiety since the Waldbaum blaze. Except for one, all said they did not believe they could return to active duty because of their psychological scars.

"I could never go into another burning building," said 30-year-old Hal Plaut. He told of dreaming "I'm burning, my house is burning. I have installed smoke detectors everywhere. Often in the middle of the night, I wake up and check the stove."

The men also said their mental problems have caused severe strains on their family life.

One fireman, John Madigan, told of how he complained of chest pains for two months and was told nothing was wrong and was ordered on light duty. He went to a heart specialist who operated on him that afternoon.

"He was almost in shock," said the surgeon, Dr. Emile A. Naclerio, adding that the firefighter is now close to becoming a "chronic invalid."

Richard Vizzini, president of the Uniformed Firefighters Assn., yesterday had sent a telegram to Mayor Koch urging he intercede see that "these men get proper care."

Vizzini noted that union has complained years about the treatment in the Medical Dept. that in their latest contract they won the right to set a medical practices review committee.

Slow-motion bureaucracy

What is it about the officials who run this city that requires that they be pushed and prodded day after day before they move even tentatively to correct the most glaring faults in the way they run our affairs?

Just over three weeks ago The Post published details of the psychological damage being suffered by the heroic firemen who survived the roof collapse in the ghastly Brooklyn supermarket blaze last August in which six of their comrades perished.

We called for full-scale help from Mayor Koch in overturning the rebuffs they had been dealt in seeking medical treatment through the Fire Dept.

Yesterday, after further prolonged, unnecessary suffering, Fire Commissioner Augustus A. Beekman ordered a reevaluation of the medical diagnosis and treatment provided.

"There are neither monetary nor administrative reasons for denying these men any required medical treatment," he reported to the Mayor. Why, then, the delay? Why, quite simply, was it not possible to do the obvious at once when the obvious was so clearly indicated?

From The New York Post, 12/13/78. Reprinted with permission.

XXXXXXXXXXXXXXXXXXXXXXXXXXXXXXXXXXXXXXXXXXXXXXXXXXXXXXXXXXXXXXX

After reading these articles you may ask, "How could the Fire Department be so unsympathetic toward these men?" The closest I can come to an explanation is an educated guess:

I think it was the first time members requested psychological help because they felt they could not go back to work, and there simply was no provision for it. It was easier to give some more time off and hope that they bounce back.

If such help was requested in 1966 when 12 men were lost in the 23rd Street fire, I wouldn't know. I was not on the job at that time. Requested or not, surely a few required it.

Money, of course, plays a part here. Long-term psychotherapy is expensive and not always successful. It's cheaper just to give time off.

Herein is the logic in CISD teams: By getting to the scene of a critical incident as soon as possible (not later than the following day), the emotional trauma, if any, can be treated early and possibly decrease time lost on medical leaves or prevent an early retirement.

NOTE: The previous paragraph is a simplification in the author's words and should not be construed as a clinical definition.
See Appendix for access to more info on CISD.

Ladder 102/Engine 209 logo and shoulder patch

courtesy of Firefighter John Kiernan

XXX

compassion \kem-'pash-en\ n: *sympathetic consciousness of others' distress together with a desire to alleviate it*
Webster's 7th New Collegiate Dictionary

PART 8

"FINAL REPORT"

One night on a late watch in Ladder Co. 102 (my first assigned unit), I gazed out the front of the firehouse during an unusual quiet spell. Everyone else was upstairs in the dormitory waiting for the inevitable call. As I looked up and down Bedford Avenue, I thought about the system of which I was a small part.

At any time, never knowing exactly when, we will be ordered to respond to a call for help. As the housewatchman, I would receive the call by telephone or (at the time) telegraph bell signal. Then I would flip a switch, press two or three buttons, and announce the location to everyone via the intercom.

XXXXXXXXXXXXXXXXXXXXXXXXXXXXXXXXXXXXXXXXXXXXXXXXXXXXXXXXXXXXXXX

In less than one minute, about a dozen men on three vehicles (ladder, pumper and chief's car) would be out the door. En route, as more information came over the radio, each member would automatically size up the situation by drawing upon his past training and experience.

The *size-up would determine what action to take in accordance with specifically assigned duties for that tour. Sometimes the additional information is a report of people trapped. Even though searches for victims are routinely made anyway, hearing that people are trapped sharpens the focus of the primary objective, which is to save the victims before the fire claims them.

What a great system! What a noble profession! What an awesome responsibility! Sometimes the pressures of that responsibility can seem too much to bear, especially when the fire wins the race. Then, who will save the saviors?

*For structural fires, the size-up is an evaluation taking into account such factors including, but not limited to, the time of day, the weather, potential occupancy (residential, commercial, school, office, factory, hospital, etc.), type of construction (wood frame, brick, high-rise, etc.). Then there are non-structural fires and emergencies such as vehicular collisions, gas leaks, power lines down, stuck elevators, etc., etc., etc.

XXXXXXXXXXXXXXXXXXXXXXXXXXXXXXXXXXXXXXXXXXXXXXXXXXXXXXXXXXXXXX

After leaving the Department in 1989, I visited most of my old firehouses several times. Among the new faces at Ladder 153, there were still some members I had worked with back in the latter '70s. Over a cup of coffee, we would talk about how the job is changing or what it's like to be retired or whatever. Invariably, if Richie Frizzel was there, I'd get a little verbal hazing.

Hazing is a somewhat strange firehouse tradition. Usually directed at the newer members, no one is immune; not even the captain, unless he has no sense of humor at all. It's nothing more than good, clean fun during the lulls between alarms. Some might say it will be a lost art, now that Danny Rogers retired.

One day it occurred to me that most members assigned to Ladder 153 and Engine 254 were not even on the job at the time of the Waldbaums fire. I presumed their only exposure to the incident was via training drills on "truss collapse."

Here were young firefighters actually walking in the foot-steps of George Rice and Jim McManus and I didn't think they had an adequate perception of what it was like to be a fire-fighter at the time of the Waldbaums fire. So, I prepared a scrapbook of

XXXXXXXXXXXXXXXXXXXXXXXXXXXXXXXXXXXXXXXXXXXXXXXXXXXXXXXXXXXXXXX

news articles (similar to Part 4) and presented it to the company so they and future members may be aware of some of their firehouse's history.

Following is the cover letter to that scrapbook. Although directed to one firehouse, its message applies to firefighters everywhere:

XXXXXXXXXXXXXXXXXXXXXXXXXXXXXXXXXXXXXXXXXXXXXXXXXXXXXXXXXXXXX

XXX

August 2, 1991

Dear Firefighter,

The following copies of newspaper clippings and photos document the Waldbaums fire of August 2, 1978.

In the history of the Fire Department of New York, it is a major event deserving of your attention.

For the families of the 6 men killed, it was (and always will be) devastating.

For their brother firefighters, whether on duty or not, the feelings of loss and helplessness were overwhelming.

I pray that you never experience such a loss. I also pray that you never have to carry a lifeless body from a fire, but I'm afraid that's too much to ask for in this business.

As a firefighter, you see yourself as a protector of others; never as a victim in need of help. It is therefore inherent that you can't or won't ask for help when needed. This does not mean that all firefighters are hardheads; it's just that you'd rather pass up help to someone who "really" needs it.

This innate quality in firefighters has finally been officially recognized by the Administration via the recommendations of the professionals in the field of mental health. This is why FDNY now has a Crisis Response Team.

They can't teach you in probie school how to cope with multiple fatalities (whether civilian or uniformed) but there is now help available when needed. Make no mistake; whether you carry dozens of bodies or just one child or a brother firefighter, you are a victim of a horrible experience and in need of much support.

Fraternally,

Ernest F. DiMaria

Ernest F. DiMaria
Ret. Lt., FDNY

XXXXXXXXXXXXXXXXXXXXXXXXXXXXXXXXXXXXXXXXXXXXXXXXXXXXXXXXXXXXXXXXXX

As I indicated briefly in Part 3, the effects of stress on rescue personnel were either ignored or underestimated. Nothing much more than allowing time to pass was officially done, even though an incident might have been so overwhelming that the rescuers, in effect, became victims as well.

In the latter part of 1989, the FDNY announced its plan for a "Crisis Response Team" to tend to the psychological needs of members involved in unusually tragic incidents. And I might add, not a moment too soon, as it was first utilized after an arsonist set fire to the Happy Land Social Club in the Bronx on March 25, 1990.

It was the largest mass murder in America. In a senseless act of vengeance against a woman, he set fire to the building with total disregard for any of the occupants. Ironically, the woman survived, but 87 people died within minutes from smoke asphyxiation and panic. None were burned.

Upon arrival of the firefighting units, the fire itself was the least of their problems and it was extinguished routinely. The operation was mainly that of body count and identification of victims in coordination with Emergency Medical Services (EMS) and the Police Department.

XXXXXXXXXXXXXXXXXXXXXXXXXXXXXXXXXXXXXXXXXXXXXXXXXXXXXXXXXXXXXXXX

Members of all ranks were deeply distressed by what they saw:

"There is nothing that can prepare you for the incident I just witnessed."
>Assistant Chief Frank Nastro,
>Citywide Command Chief on Duty

"They say that time heals all wounds. This may be true, but the scars remain forever."
>Firefighter Craig Buccieri
>Ladder Co. 33

The above quotes were taken from WNYF Magazine (2nd issue of 1990) which featured a story of the Happy Land Social Club fire.

Rather than one member (usually a chief officer), writing for WNYF about the incident, five members expressed their views and how it affected them. After reading it, I never felt worse about no longer being an active member of the New York City Fire Department. I also felt proud as ever, to have been part of it.

I think the article accomplished a great deal to help elimi-nate the stigma of sensitivity to tragedy as a sign of weakness. When a respected veteran chief officer of the FDNY admits to tears,

XXXXXXXXXXXXXXXXXXXXXXXXXXXXXXXXXXXXXXXXXXXXXXXXXXXXXXXXXXXXX

that is not weakness; it is compassion, which is a trait of all persons of worth. I can't say that firefighters have more compassion than others, but due to the nature of their work, they experience it more often.

If you (the reader) are involved in rescue work, I would hope that your department has a program for stress de-briefing or at least access to one. One of the most important aspects of such a program is its confidentiality, and it may well make the difference between coping with your job and leaving it.

Getting back to the Waldbaums fire, I chose as a logical conclusion, an article from Firehouse Magazine, written by Vincent Dunn, whose book, "Collapse of Burning Buildings," was used as a reference in Part 1.

The article *"Truss Collapse: Final Report" is reprinted as follows:

(c) With permission of Firehouse Magazine

XXXXXXXXXXXXXXXXXXXXXXXXXXXXXXXXXXXXXXXXXXXXXXXXXXXXXXXXXXXXXXX

Lessons learned from the fatal Waldbaum's fire.

Truss Collapse: Final Report

By VINCENT DUNN

Power saws are used to ventilate supermarket roof. The "rain roof" shielded firefighters from fire and hindered roof ventilation.

Editor's Note: In one of the most tragic fires in the history of the New York City Fire Department, six firefighters were killed and dozens of others injured during a four-alarm fire in a Waldbaum's supermarket in the Sheepshead Bay section of Brooklyn on August 2, 1978. Thirty-two minutes after the first units arrived, 24 firefighters were operating on the building's timber truss roof when it suddenly collapsed, plunging the six men to their deaths. One hundred fifty firefighters manning 26 engines and ladders and the city's four rescue companies battled the blaze (see "On The Job: Brooklyn," Firehouse, September 1978).

I had worked a night tour, and while trying to sleep the morning out, I was awakened by a radio report of a Brooklyn building collapse, in which a group of firefighters was buried. Like many other firefighters, I immediately drove out to the fire, to lend a hand, if it were needed, or, in the way that families come together in times of crisis, just to be there.

I remember seeing journalists at the scene, walking back and forth in front of the still smoldering building, doing their job, trying to gather all the facts. Columnists Murray Kempton and Jimmy Breslin were there, among others. The fire chiefs of the FDNY were huddled together in a firehouse just two blocks away, putting the pieces together, trying to find answers to the questions the fire commissioner and mayor would ask.

I was asking myself about what I saw, and what I knew. The most fundamental question was, How did it happen? The next was, Why? I remember feeling there was a great lesson in this fire for all of us, one that we should never forget, whether firefighters or chiefs, and that is we have a life-and-death need, and a life-and-death responsibility, to know as much as we possibly can about fighting fires. When there is something we don't know, fires like the one at Waldbaum's happen.

The Waldbaum's fire brought about

increased awareness of the hazards of operating on and near truss roofs. As a result of the incident, much information was published on the subject to alert firefighters nationwide about the quick collapse potential of this type of structure, greatly changing firefighting strategy.

We present the following story by Firehouse Contributing Editor Vincent Dunn, FDNY deputy chief and recognized authority on building collapse, who gives his personal reflections on the incident and explains why it occurred and how it has affected the fire service.

—Dennis Smith

When I heard on the morning of August 2, 1978, that six firefighters had died in a timber truss roof collapse at a burning Brooklyn supermarket, I asked myself some very disturbing questions: What did I know about truss roofs? Not enough to have ordered the men off the roof before it collapsed. Would those six men have died if I were the chief-in-com-

As ventilation continued, 24 firefighters operated on roof prior to collapse of truss roof. Twelve men fell in; six were killed.

mand of that fire? Yes, they would have.

I remember that after the incident I looked through two books on firefighting strategy and noted that both mentioned truss roof construction and its collapse danger very briefly, with only a few lines of warning. (Francis Brannigan's book *Building Construction for the Fire Service* covered the subject more thoroughly.) Then I tried to recall my experience with timber truss roofs in my 20 years of firefighting. My earliest recollection was in the late 1950s when our company was inspecting an old auto parking garage, and our captain pointed to the open underside of the roof and said that the roof was dangerous. I remember seeing crossed wood truss web members at the underside of a very high roof. Then, when I was a backstep firefighter in the early 1960s, a fire occurred in an old vacant movie theater on my day off. Responding firefighters talked about the collapse of its timber truss roof the next day. Ten years later, a classmate in a college night course told me about a timber truss roof collapse that had occurred the day be-

fore, showing me a photograph of a building with a large opening in the roof.

In my years of firefighting and academic and promotional study of fire protection, those few instances were my only contact with the timber truss roof—one of the most dangerous structures that exists from a firefighting point of view. It would not have been enough to influence my strategy if I had commanded the Waldbaum's fire. Today I know quite a lot about truss roofs, but at the time I asked myself how I could, in good conscience, command an operation and be responsible for the lives of other firefighters if I had such little knowledge of collapse dangers.

After the collapse, one of the charges brought against the City of New York and the New York Fire Department was that none of the department's written training material mentioned the subject of truss roof collapse (*see accompanying box*). The lawyers stated that this was a failure of the municipality to properly train its employees. Looking back, I find it hard to believe that, with the tremen-

dous amount of bulletins, circulars and directives issued to the department by the division of training, a subject as important as truss roofs was never covered. But it was not, nor were many other collapse dangers that firefighters confront. The fire department training division now supplies a considerable amount of printed information on truss roofs and other collapse dangers.

The city and the FDNY were also criticized for not providing formal training to chief officers. In my case, when I entered the fire department in 1957 and served as a probationary firefighter, I received three months of training. As a newly promoted company officer in 1963, I received six weeks of instruction. But when I was promoted to chief officer in 1973 I received no training. This pattern is typical for chiefs throughout most of the U.S: Training is almost nonexistent, primarily because local governments cannot justify the cost of training small groups of chiefs, and very few chief officers are qualified and willing to teach fire strategy and tactics.

Today, the city provides training to FDNY chiefs through a chief officer's development program. Chiefs attend conferences where they are encouraged to exchange information about firefighting strategy, tactics and fireground safety and discuss the latest life safety and fire protection innovations. The National Fire Academy at Emmitsburg, Maryland, assists New York with the costly burden of training chiefs through its two-week course on fireground strategy and tactics, "Command and Control of Fire Department Major Operations." Designed for battalion chiefs and tour commanders, the course provides chiefs with a nationwide overall view of the role of the fireground commander and operations at fires and emergencies. The course, held at the National Emergency Training Center, prevents the danger of "inbreeding" and a "know-it-all" attitude that can develop among firefighters in large or small fire departments where members receive only limited in-house training.

The final report of the fire department's investigation into the Waldbaum

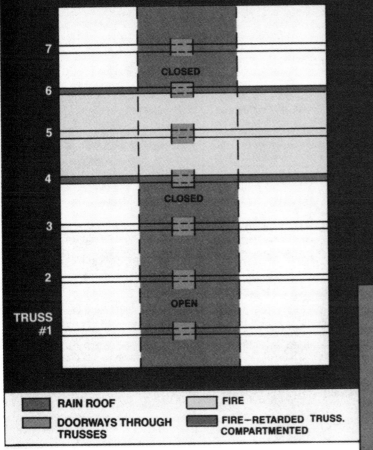

7

CLOSED

6

5

4

CLOSED

3

2

OPEN

TRUSS #1

RAIN ROOF

DOORWAYS THROUGH TRUSSES

FIRE

FIRE-RETARDED TRUSS. COMPARTMENTED

RAIN ROOF ↓

DOOR OPENING THROUGH TRUSS

roof collapse stated that the firefighters had died partly because "the extent, the severity and to some extent the location of the fire had not been clearly defined prior to the collapse." One of the most important size-up duties of first-in chiefs and company officers is locating the fire and determining its severity. This information lays the foundation for the entire operation. First, it determines the amount of firefighters and equipment needed to control the blaze. Second, until the location and extent of the fire are known, firefighters cannot determine the overall life hazard, the most effective point of fire attack, and the most efficient method of venting heat and smoke.

Roof Collapse: A Legal Perspective

By BART MITCHELL

The lawsuit involving the Waldbaum's supermarket fire was settled in November of 1985. A total of $13.5 million was awarded to the widows of the six firefighters and to the firefighters injured in the incident. Contributing to the settlement figure were Waldbaum's, insurance companies, the City of New York, architects, subcontractors, electricians and the owner of the property. The New York law firm of Lipsig, Sullivan & Liapakis, P.C. acted as head counsel in the case.

The painstaking investigatory work of fire marshals assigned to the case yielded clues that would later help the law firm's own investigators, experts and attorneys to piece together the factors that contributed to the unanticipated collapse of the roof. These factors were the basis of the theories of liabilitiy against the defendants in the case.

Truss Construction

The supermarket was a one-story non-fireproof building originally constructed in 1952. Along the north side of the building workmen had substantially completed work on an extension to the supermarket. The roof was of a bowstring truss design consisting of seven wooden trusses running the width of the building, north to south.

The advantage of a truss roof is the elimination of interior support columns. However, the truss design is inherently dangerous because of its high susceptibility to early collapse when exposed to fire, as compared to other roof designs. When attacked by flame, an entire truss may collapse following the failure of a single web member.

Improper Training

Up until the time of collapse, however, none of the chief officers on the roof realized the danger because they had never been formally instructed to recognize truss roofs or the significance of their design weakness (although reference to the dangers of truss roofs had been published in books on fire tactics). The City of New York was sued be-

Bart Mitchell, an associate of the law firm Lipsig, Sullivan & Liapakis, P.C., is the son of an FDNY battalion chief.

cause prior to the collapse, none of its All Unit Circulars, Training Bulletins, Safety Bulletins, Rules and Regulations, Fire Communications Manual, Standard Operating procedures, Division Circulars, Directives or other materials circulated to its personnel ever mentioned the subject of truss roofs or their dangers. While the city could not be held liable for an error in judgment in the course of fighting a fire, New York law says the failure of a municipality to properly train its employees may lead to the imposition of liability on the municipality.

Attic and Cockloft

There were several other factors in the design and construction of the supermarket which led to its premature collapse. The building code in effect in 1951, the year in which the original building plans were submitted, required that "attic" space had to be firestopped at a maximum of 2500 square feet. The plans called for firestopping only on every other truss, 2, 4, 6. Although the space between truss 4 and 6 was almost 4000 square feet, the plans were approved. There was no fire stopping on truss 5, which failed first, pulling down a large section of the roof with it. Also, any containment of the fire which might have been provided by truss 4, the one between the point of origin of the fire and truss 5, was defeated by the construction workers who tied open the doors in the cockloft for their convenience. This evidence pointed to negligence on the part of the original owners, designers and builders, as well as the city for approving plans in violation of the building code.

Breach in the Ceiling

Adding the extension necessitated doing work on the north wall of the supermarket. Alteration plans called for the eventual removal of the north wall and lally columns supporting the bottom chords of trusses 2 to 6. These trusses would then be supported by steel columns located inside the extension. Courses of brick and cement block were removed along the top of the north wall to expose the underside of trusses 2 and 6. To facilitate their ac-

cess to these work areas however, several courses of brick and block were removed along the wall, exposing a much wider area between trusses 2 and 6 than was necessary. This created an uninhibited flow of air between the extension and the mezzanine area where the fire was started. In the mezzanine itself, a hole was cut in the ceiling and a 4 x 4 was wedged between the floor of the mezzanine and the bottom chord of truss 4. While it was of little or no value in supporting the massive bulk of the truss, fire marshals theorized that it was from the base of this 4 x 4 that the fire had spread through the breach into the structure of the roof.

Suspended Ceiling

In addition to the hazard created by these violations, the firefighters were frustrated in the attempts to define the location and extent of the fire from both below and above. The original metal ceiling, attached to the bottom chords of the trusses, was 16 feet high. Subsequently, an acoustical tile ceiling was suspended approximately 18 inches below the original ceiling. No plans for this suspended ceiling were on file, and its unanticipated presence complicated attempts to pull the high ceiling.

Double Roof

Above the fire, venting teams were confronted by a double roof which had been constructed over a sizeable area of the original roof. No plans had ever been filed for this "rain roof," which delayed the venting teams and prevented the observation of the tell-tale signs of radiating heat, melting roofing materials and sponginess, while the fire was raging below.

Every firefighter is aware of the risks inherent in his job, and accepts them. Generally, the courts recognize these inherent risks and will not impose liability on a defendant for the injuries that result unless he has created or tolerated an unreasonably unsafe condition. This applies to construction sites as well as finished structures. But when the regulations designed to protect firefighters and the general public are violated, the courts will compensate those who have suffered injuries.

Sometimes, however, the location and severity of a fire cannot be assessed by the chiefs and company officers first on the scene. This is often due to alterations or unusual construction of the fire building. In a fire that killed 12 FDNY firefighters in 1966, the exact location of the fire was not discovered due to alterations. Similarly, the severity and extent of the Brooklyn supermarket fire was not "clearly defined" due to three factors: an unusual alteration called a "rain roof," the fire-retarding compartmentation of the trusses and the large heat collection space created by the bowstring design of the structure.

Rain roof. Because the supermarket's bowstring roof was sagging and rainwater was accumulating at its depressed center, a second roof, or "rain roof," had been built over its center. The rain roof recreated the curve at the highest point of the roof and enabled water to roll to the sides of the trusses, where scuppers and drains removed it to the street. The rain roof was not simply another layer of tar paper placed on top of the original roof, nor was it a so-called "raised" or "inverted" roof, where the roof deck is built up on a flat roof by placing 2- by 4-inch wood members on top of roof beams and a single deck atop the wood members. Instead, the rain roof at the Brooklyn supermarket consisted of wood beams and a roof deck laid on top of the old tar roof. There were two roof decks, then, which acted as an insulating barrier between the fire and the men on the roof and also delayed roof venting. When firefighters cut the top rain roof with a power saw and pulled up the plywood deck with hooks and halligan tools, they discovered another roof deck beneath this. To accomplish ventilation, they had to cut another, smaller opening within the original opening. The rain roof had been laid down the center or highest point of the curved roof, where the heat and fire below were the greatest.

Fire-retarding compartmentation. Inside the large enclosed roof space of the supermarket were seven bowstring wood timber trusses spaced 20 feet apart. A door opening was located at the center of each bowstring truss, with a walkway providing access through each truss from the front to the rear of the large roof space. Truss numbers 2, 4 and 6 were fire retarded and covered with one-hour plasterboard. Held open by a fusible link, the automatic fire doors would close automatically when the link was melted by fire. Trusses 1, 3, 5 and 7 were exposed, unprotected wood trusses.

When the fire extended from the mezzanine floor into the large roof space, it spread between trusses 4, 5 and 6. The automatic fire doors closed on trusses 4 and 6, confining the flames between

Memorial to the six firefighters killed at Waldbaum's at the FDNY Training Academy.

those trusses. The fire grew on both sides of truss 5, which eventually collapsed. A 4000-square-foot section of roof deck fell with it, the roof deck split apart, and fire roared out into the 40- by 100-foot crevice. Twelve firefighters tumbled into this fire-filled trench. Miraculously, six fell through to the floor of the supermarket and were able to make their way to safety. Six others were burned to death; the bodies of several of them were found on top of the display shelves.

Because the fire was confined between trusses 4, 5 and 6, there was little or no indication of fire when firefighters pulled down the ceiling beyond this area. When they looked up into the roof space, they saw no sign of fire, so they had to open the ceiling between trusses 4 or 6. The same confusing effect occurred when roof vent openings were cut. When firefighters made the cut between trusses 3 and 4, they saw little evidence of heat or fire. When they made the next cut several feet away between trusses 4 and 6, a raging fire exploded through the vent opening.

Bowstring truss roof design. The height of the truss roof space above the ceiling in the supermarket was 10 feet at the center, and the distance from the floor to the ceiling inside the store was 16 feet. Thus, the total distance from floor to underside of the truss roof was 26 feet. The fire started in the mezzanine floor, burned upward past a double ceiling and spread out into a large roof space. Ordinarily when a firefighter enters a burning room with an 8- or 10-foot-high ceiling, the distance the heat and smoke are banked down below the ceiling is one of the factors used in determining the severity of the fire. The lower the firefighter is forced to crouch down to escape the heat, the more serious the fire. Converse-

ly, if a firefighter can walk upright, the fire is considered small or not serious.

In an occupancy with a high ceiling or a bowstring truss roof space that can collect a lot of heat and fire, firefighters can be misled about the severity of the fire. There may be two conflicting statements about the fire's size and severity: Firefighters on the roof, after venting the fire, will report a serious fire; meanwhile, a firefighter walking upright underneath the heat and flame may report a fire of little severity. In a fire department with a history of interior firefighting, like New York City, the report from inside the fire building is often considered the most accurate report of fire severity. However, at a truss roof building or a structure with a high ceiling where crew members give conflicting reports, the roof report of a serious fire may be the most accurate assessment.

Conclusion. Waldbaum's was not the first bowstring truss roof that collapsed in the 120-year history of the New York City Fire Department. After the Brooklyn supermarket collapse, chiefs, company officers and firefighters came forward and related many past incidents of truss roof collapses. Somehow, though, these fires had not been documented or made known to chiefs at any training conferences. Only the chiefs and officers assigned to areas that included older industrial and manufacturing buildings (such as the Hunt's Point section of the Bronx and Greenpoint section of Brooklyn) were aware of the dangers of truss roofs. The Waldbaum's supermarket, on the other hand, was built in 1952 in a predominantly residential area.

Over the years, the fire service has expended little effort to document and record its firefighting experience. Though we have developed extensive preplanning procedures to prepare for all types of fires and emergencies, we have not adequately explored the advantages of postfire analysis—examining a fire operation after it occurs from the perspective of strategy, tactics and fireground survival. For years, insurance companies have conducted investigations of fires after they occurred, but always from a property protection point of view. The fire service should consider analyzing significant fires by documenting them on fact sheets, diagramming the fire building and photographing the fire scene after the operation. This information could then be distributed throughout the fire department or to the entire fire service, if it is of great significance.

If the knowledge and experience of the earlier truss roof collapses had been communicated to all chiefs and company officers in the city, perhaps the Waldbaum's supermarket collapse would not have been fatal.

Data On Total Fire Personnel And
Fire Fighter Fatalities 1978-1991

Year	Total Fire Personnel [1]	Fire Fighter Fatalities [2]
1978	287,166	74
1979	308,638	70
1980	308,382	98
1981	312,136	73
1982	310,270	48
1983	309,670	42
1984	16,212	40
1985	316,540	34
1986	325,686	25
1987	335,020	31
1988	340,343	46
1989	316,723	47
1990	327,121	34
1991	341,371	32

Source:

[1]: Public Employment 1978-1991; Bureau of the Census

[2]: Department of Occupational Safety and Health, International Association of Fire Fighters

(Statistics do not reflect volunteer personnel)

xxxxxxxxxxxxxxxxxxxxxxxxxxxxxxxxxxxxxxxxxxxxxxxxxxxxxxxxxxxxxxxxx

XXX

"You don't want the fire to win"

Capt. Martin McTigue

Rescue Co. 4

PART 9

"EPILOGUE"

On a somewhat brighter note, the fatality rate among fire-fighters has declined since 1978. In addition to an increased awareness of potential collapse, there have been concentrated efforts toward safety training for all ranks. Experience is a great teacher, but training is forever. The art of firefighting demands it.

During my last visit to NYC (Oct. '92), I noted a newspaper clipping posted on a firehouse bulletin board. It was about a fire in Brooklyn at which the chief ordered all personnel out of a building. Seconds later there was a collapse that might have had tragic results. Based on his experience and training, that order saved an unknown number of firefighters from possible death or maiming.

XXXXXXXXXXXXXXXXXXXXXXXXXXXXXXXXXXXXXXXXXXXXXXXXXXXXXXXXXXXXX

Firefighters do not like being ordered out of a building, because it is tantamount to losing the battle and it will take longer to get the fire under control. One night in 1980, while assigned to Engine 34 in Manhattan, we responded to a fire that was already going strong. A broken plate glass window on the ground floor of the building was allowing plenty of air in to feed it.

Because of a hydrant problem, there was a delay in getting water. Although the delay was less than a minute, the fire intensified greatly, and the radiant heat from the building seared the polyester jacket (covering) off the hose that was laid out on the sidewalk.

Inside the window to the left, I noticed that the fire was burning quite vigorously. A broken gas pipe was causing the flames to shoot several feet up like an oversized blow torch.

Somewhere, in the thousands of pages I studied, I read that it was safer to have escaping gas burn off than to let it accumulate into an explosive mixture. Nevertheless, I took comfort in knowing that an emergency crew from the utility company would soon be there to shut off the supply and make sure it *stayed* off.

XXXXXXXXXXXXXXXXXXXXXXXXXXXXXXXXXXXXXXXXXXXXXXXXXXXXXXXXXXXXXXX

Finally, we got water in the line and entered the building, extinguishing fire along the way, further and further in, like an advancing infantry killing the enemy. Because of the severity and extent of the fire, we needed a back-up line but it was not coming because the chief was ordering everybody out.

When I relayed the order to the men on the line, my nozzle-man asked for "two more minutes" to stop the fire from spreading to the floor above.

Well, actually he said, "Lieu, two more minutes and we got this motherfucker!" He didn't think we were in imminent danger and neither did I, but from our position, we couldn't possibly know the overall situation. I also didn't think it was possible to knock down the fire in two minutes without another line. Furthermore, he would not have to explain to the chief why we stayed in there in defiance of his order. I ordered him out.

Without an interior attack on the fire, some floors eventually collapsed. But there were no injuries or close calls; just a disgruntled firefighter who disagreed with a command decision.

* * *

XXXXXXXXXXXXXXXXXXXXXXXXXXXXXXXXXXXXXXXXXXXXXXXXXXXXXXXXXXXXXXXX

Yes, training is forever. But no amount of training can prevent death and injuries if the firefighters are not informed of unusual situations or alterations, such as the "rain roof."
(See page 163)

As to why the Fire Department wasn't informed of the unstable roof, a New York Post editorial stated that it was "puzzling." (See page 75) Some questions have no satisfactory answers.

Firefighters have many puzzling questions with no satisfactory answers. As you read this, fire hydrants are obstructed by parked vehicles, false alarms are transmitted, cigarettes are carelessly discarded, and children are left unattended. "Why?"
There are many excuses but no satisfactory answers.

*   *   *

For days after the Waldbaums fire, we walked around in shock. Imagine the bewilderment of the children too young to understand what had happened to their fathers.   Almost all the children are adults now, forever to carry the heartbreaking but proud legacy left by their dads.

*   *   *

XXXXXXXXXXXXXXXXXXXXXXXXXXXXXXXXXXXXXXXXXXXXXXXXXXXXXXXXXXXXX

BEFORE CLOSING ...

In 1992 I traveled to New York in February and October. During my February visit, a fire took the life of Lieutenant Thomas A. Williams of Rescue 4. From the fire scene, Williams was rushed to Elmhurst General Hospital and FDNY Chaplain Mychal Judge was notified. Upon arrival at the emergency room, Father Judge had to administer the last rites to Lt. Williams. This was later described as a "baptism of fire" for Father Judge, because it was his first day as a newly appointed FDNY chaplain.

I was at the quarters of Engine Company 321, my last assigned unit, when the dreaded 5-5-5-5 came over the Voice Alarm. The "four fives" are a carryover from the bell telegraph days, but the message is the same:

"The signal 5-5-5-5 has been transmitted ... Stand by for Department message." (Repeat) "It is with regret ... that announcement is made ... of the death of ... (Rank, Name and Unit) ... which occurred at (time and date) ... while operating at (location)."

After three years in retirement, what were the chances of hearing that message again?

XXXXXXXXXXXXXXXXXXXXXXXXXXXXXXXXXXXXXXXXXXXXXXXXXXXXXXXXXXXXXXXXX

On the day of Lt. Williams' funeral, the town of Kings Park, NY could barely handle the influx of traffic. Kings Park is among scores of towns and villages within suburban Suffolk County; each one proud of its own fire stations. You can bet that every department in the county was represented. One estimate was as high as 10,000 mourners.

On October 14, 1992, at the FDNY Memorial Day Service, the widow of Lt. Thomas Williams accepted his medal. Well over 2000 members of FDNY stood in formation on Riverside Drive that day, but not one could guess that less than a month later, (11/10), Rescue 4 would almost lose another member of their unit, their captain, Martin McTigue.

Burns from a steam explosion resulted in a 12- week stay at the NYC Burn Center for Capt. McTigue. *On the following page is a clipping from The New York Times published one week after his release.

The stories of Lt. Williams and Capt. McTigue were included here because they fit the premise of this book most vividly; that fire is truly a war that never ends.

* * * * * *

*See New York Times article (Feb. 8, 1993) on page 173.

XXXXXXXXXXXXXXXXXXXXXXXXXXXXXXXXXXXXXXXXXXXXXXXXXXXXXXXXXXXXXXXXX

XX

Hailing Grit of an Injured Firefighter

By DOUGLAS MARTIN

A year ago at a funeral, a husky firefighter introduced himself to Patricia McTigue and said: "I admire your husband. He's everything I'm striving to be."

She next saw the firefighter on Tuesday, when he was watching from the curb as her husband — his 6-foot-1 body savagely transmogrified by burns that eight operations have only begun to heal — was released from the hospital. He gave a thumbs-up sign.

"He's just somebody who needs a hero," Fire Capt. Martin McTigue said of his colleague, managing to make a slight smile though not managing to make it seem easy.

We all need heroes, and it was so profoundly apparent on Tuesday when Captain McTigue was released from the burn unit of New York Hospital-Cornell Medical Center.

He had been in the hospital since November 1992, after suffering severe burns when he was caught in a blast of steam responding to an explosion at the Consolidated Edison Plant in Manhattan.

For Captain McTigue's release on Tuesday, there were speeches, crowds and a white stretch limousine to take him home to Baldwin, L.I. A police escort and bagpipes, too.

All this was immensely appreciated, but for this 48-year-old child of Brooklyn, things hit home when his motorcade passed the Learn About Nursery School where his four daugh-

---

'We have all conquered death,' says the captain.

---

ters, now ages 14 to 21, had learned to print their names. Today's children screeched, jumped wildly and waved a big banner. It was precisely then that he comprehended.

"This is really something special," he said he thought at the time. "This is more than I expected."

What Captain McTigue realized was that people, on a fundamental level, were also celebrating themselves, celebrating the miracle of surviving another day, celebrating the inescapable truth that we are all in the same boat.

"They were just feeling good about being alive, and I really believe we have all conquered death in some sort of way," he said in a whispery gritty voice caused by the burns inside his lungs. "It was a form of love."

Not that Captain McTigue ever aspired to special mention. Indeed, Firefighter Frank McCabe, who grew up with him and is now a department spokesman after being injured in a fire, noted that Captain McTigue, until his accident, had never received an official commendation for his courage. "Say, he rescued a baby," he said. "He'd come out and hand it to somebody and walk away."

Bags of Letters

Now Captain McTigue is at home, a comfortable two-story place where the needlepoint asks God to "Bless This House" and the many framed photographs are of generations of family. His first fire helmet, which began to leak after years of wear, hangs on the wall in the den. Letters of support fill brown grocery bags.

He has begun physical therapy in the neighborhood, besides returning to New York Hospital once a week, Since his wife works and his daughters are gone much of the time, he is often alone.

He is hardly singular. In 1991, the International Association of Fire Fighters says, 93,963 of the nation's 225,000 career firefighters suffered some form of injury. There were 32 deaths from injuries in the line of duty, while 31 firefighters died from occupational diseases like exposure to chemicals or stress.

Captain McTigue's previous serious injury was two and a half years ago, when another firefighter fell through two floors and landed on Captain McTigue's head. Six of his teeth were broken. He has been painfully burned more times than he can recall. "It's pretty easy to get injured at a fire," he said.

He grew up in the Flatbush section of Brooklyn, one of "tons of kids" who delighted in doing one thing for a week or two, then something else for the next. There was a time when everyone was making rickety vehicles from old rollerskates and fruit cartons. Then there was stoop ball, roasting potatoes in a vacant lot, and on one magical long ago afternoon, seeing Hopalong Cassidy on a white horse at Ebbets Field.

Marty McTigue always knew what he wanted to be. His high school yearbook had nothing more than this to say about him: "Hopes to become a New York City Firefighter."

At 17, he went to work in the Brooklyn Navy Yard, contributing in this way to the Vietnam War. He had wanted to fight, until he saw too much of it on television. When the yard wound down, he was sent to the yard at Norfolk, Va., to build more ships.

When that ended in 1965, the city transit police were hiring, so he took the test and did that for four years. The experience heightened his ambition to be a firefighter. It is the perilous uncertainty of police work that he found unsettling, the realization that anybody might be a killer. For a firefighter, by contrast, fire itself is the only enemy and all people deserve to be rescued.

"No matter how bad a person might be, in a fire he is just a person who needs help," he said.

Then came the evening of Nov. 10, 1992.

It was 10 or so, just as the firefighters of Queens Rescue Company No. 4 were finishing a leisurely dinner. A bell rang and the rescue unit was ordered to the Consolidated Edison plant at First Avenue and East 39th Street, where there had been an explosion.

Arriving at the plant, they were greeted by a deafening, eerily high-pitched roar. Things happened very fast, though Captain McTigue remembers details.

He and another firefighter found themselves on a metal landing looking for people. At first the gusting steam was bearable. Suddenly, it turned exceedingly hot, 500 degrees Fahrenheit. Captain McTigue somehow shoved the other firefighter to safety. But he was trapped on the landing, paralyzed by heat. "I was being baked alive," he said.

Firefighters dashed toward him only to be repelled. It seemed like hours, but in six or seven seconds his unconscious form was dragged from the immobilizing steam bath.

He came to immediately, and begged for cold water to be dumped on his body. He knew drinks were impossible until he was under a doctor's care. Pain?

"It was there," he said. "It's not so much the present pain. It's the pain you're afraid is going to come in the future."

Captain McTigue was taken to New York Hospital's burn center. He stayed conscious for hours, communicating with Mayor David N. Dinkins and the other visitors by scribbling notes. Several hours later, he passed out and entered the world of darkness in which he lived for much of the next 12 weeks. The bandages made him look like a mummy, and a tangled skein of tubes pumped things in and out of his motionless body.

He began to draw spiritual strength from the people who would come to his room to lay a hand on his back and say something. The letters also helped. "If I had to do that all on my own, I don't think I could have done it," he said.

The family came every day to see him, and held together like glue. Not everybody could handle visiting, though, particularly the firefighters. "They could put themselves in the same situation," Captain McTigue said, "and they didn't like to see it.

"It took me a long time to look in the mirror," he said. "Let's face it, nobody would trade places with me."

And now he is at home, trying to get better. He said he would hate it if his career with New York's Bravest ended this way.

"I'd like to do a little bit more," Captain McTigue said. "You don't want the fire to win."

"Copyright (c) 1993 by
The New York Times Co.
Reprinted by permission."

XXXXXX

XXXXXXXXXXXXXXXXXXXXXXXXX

173

"Sculpture Memorial To Twelve" by Ralph Feldman

Photo courtesy International Fire Fighter

Searing, painful destruction in a fiery holocaust is the perdition reserved for the damned. This thought makes the loss of these twelve men all the more ironic and bitter. Fire became their hell on earth and consumed their heroic efforts to put down that raging inferno. But, still they come, new, eager, and with a pureness of people ready to risk life and limb for others. Each one shrugs off his calling with a matter-of-fact heroism that tolerates no mincing compromise. Every firefighter realizes that his work is serving mankind.

The Twenty-third Street fire has been described with words that weep and tears that speak. We of the Fire Service will always remember it with the eternal flame—may it never go out.   ▲

From WNYF, 4th issue of 1976

XXXXXXXXXXXXXXXXXXXXXXXXXXXXXXXXXXXXXXXXXXXXXXXXXXXXXXXXXXXXXXXXXXXX

XXX

"In all our years of fighting one sneaky fire after a tricky one, this one proved, in the most devastating way, that fire is, indeed, a red devil."

William M. Feehan
Acting Chief of Department
(25 years later; 1991)

SUPPLEMENT

"THE 23rd STREET FIRE"

No historical account of the New York City Fire Department would be complete without mentioning the 23rd Street fire of October 17, 1966. (See Parts 1, 2, 4, 5 and 7.) As the worst single loss of firefighters in New York City, I fervently hope it is never outdone or repeated. All the victims were married, leaving 12 widows and 36 children.

Years ago, when I first saw the photos of the members killed at this fire, I noticed that every rank except captain was represented, from Deputy Chief Reilly, much like his counterpart DC Kruger in 1908, to Probationary Fireman Rey, who was on the job only four months.

XXXXXXXXXXXXXXXXXXXXXXXXXXXXXXXXXXXXXXXXXXXXXXXXXXXXXXXXXXXXXXXXX

XX

Rey stands out in the photos as the only one out of uniform. New members are allowed six months to obtain a dress uniform from a limited selection of tailors. It was probably still on order.

There was no captain among the fatalities, only due to a twist of fate. In a mutual exchange of tours, Lieut. Joseph Priore (covering Battalion 4) worked in Engine Co. 18 for Captain Karl Kortum. Upon notice of the collapse, Captain Kortum went to the scene, working through the night to help search for the victims; among them were four members of his unit and Lt. Priore.

For a better understanding of this event, read the following story published by WNYF Magazine in the 2nd issue of 1973:

*"Box 598" by Firefighter Joseph D'Albert

(c) With permission of NYC Fire Department

Note: For a more in-depth study of the 23rd Street fire, see Appendix under "Recommended Reading."

XXXXXXXXXXXXXXXXXXXXXXXXXXXXXXXXXXXXXXXXXXXXXXXXXXXXXXXXXX

by JOSEPH D'ALBERT
Fireman, Eng. Co. 24

October 17, 1966 was one of the darkest days in the history of the F.D.N.Y. On that day twelve members of this department were killed in the line of duty. The following account is one man's personal experience on that tragic day; the mixed emotions that bombarded him; the final crushing realization that twelve of his brother firefighters had died; and that every man's life is irrevocably tied to another's.

I got to work at 5:15 yesterday afternoon. Another Tuesday, no different than the other six days of the week to a man in my occupation. I opened my locker and carefully hung my suit in it, replacing the blue chino trousers and blue shirt that are the work clothes of a New York City Fireman. It was all so automatic. I had gone through those motions hundreds of times before. Just as hundreds of times before, I had left my family in my home in Patchogue, Long Island to initiate the uneventful hour-long ride to Engine Company 24.

THE MEN OF E. 18

When I descended the stairs it was 5:48 and the bells were sounding. It was nothing new, but the adrenalin started motivating the body of every man in the firehouse. No man ever grows completely indifferent to that sound, no matter how long they've responded to it. Box 539 clanged in and we rolled to Jane and West Fourth Streets just as Engine 18 pulled up with little Jimmy Galanaugh in the seat. Jimmy was the type of kid you always reacted to by wanting to protect because of the impression he gave of being frail. He looked so damn out of place in the seat of that huge fire engine. He had the blond good looks of a college kid, and wasn't at all the average New Yorker's idea of what a fireman should look like. It was just one more example of how appearances can be deceiving. He was good at his job, which is what really counted.

On the back step of 18's pumper were Kelly, Tepper, and the "probie," Rey. More faces I had seen innumerable times before and taken for granted, for the simple reason that people tend to consider their relationship with each other as continuous and without end. Engine 24 had worked with 18 many times before. Our men working alongside their men was an inevitable fact of all our lives. An integral part of many operations; an integral part of a pattern we call procedure.

Kelly had been assigned to our company during most of last year's, subway strike. He was never without his pipe, his books (he was always studying for the next Lieutenants' test) and a ready smile. Kelly always smiled. Not just most of the time. Always.

Tepper was a man whose face had no age stamped on it. I could never reconcile myself to the fact that he was 41, and not just on the threshhold of his thirties. He was just perpetually young. They were both, like Jimmy, two guys a person had to like.

I had only seen the "probie" Rey a few times, but his face was familiar nevertheless. All probies wear that same expression of loneliness, mixed with a tremendous eagerness. I had experienced the feeling behind that expression myself, just as every man in the department has. And that includes my buddy Toby Vetland, who was working with me tonight and reading my mind. We had the simultaneous desire to make Rey feel more comfortable, so we went over and spoke to him. Small talk and jokes. He laughed with us gratefully—but he was waiting all the time.

He was anticipating his "big fire." All probies do. They feel that once they've gone through it, and proved themselves to the men they admire, they'll finally be accepted.

He had no way of knowing that every man there always had one eye on him for his sake, not their own. They'd break him in and watch over him at the same time, until he was capable of taking care of himself.

When I was in Japan, the people had a saying about their mountain. "He who doesn't climb Mt. Fuji once is a fool. He who climbs it twice, is an even bigger fool." Only a fireman can understand the logic behind that and apply it to his breed. Each one anxiously awaits that first big fire, and when it's all over he prays that he never sees another one. This fire had been a small one and we returned to our respective quarters when it was out.

EVENING LOOKS ROUTINE

At 7:15 a complaint came in. Since I was scheduled for the detail, I signed myself out to investigate it. Combustible rubbish in a hallway at 71 Barrow Street. It turned out to be a valid complaint, so I issued a violation order to the super of the building. He was to remove the rubbish immediately.

I was on my way back to the firehouse when a civilian called to me and pointed out an open electrical box, located in his building, with the wires exposed. I would have issued another violation order except that the super of that particular building lived just a few doors out of my district, so I called Engine 18 through headquarters. Kelly turned me over to the Lieutenant Priore who told me that he'd send a man out on it right away.

When I signed myself back in quarters a few minutes later, it appeared that the evening was going to be a quiet one. A lot of routine. Not that any one of us had ever been guaranteed a completely routine evening; there are no guarantees in this job. But the overall mood of the firehouse was a quiet one.

We began our evening meal at 8:35.

E. 24 RESPONDS TO 4TH

At 9:36 Box 598 came in. At 9:58 the 'All hands' came in, which meant that the companies that responded to that first alarm had a fire and were hard at work. We checked the response card. Engine 18 was scheduled to respond on the second alarm and we had to go on the fourth. It didn't necessarily mean that there would even be a second, third, or fourth alarm. But we stood by.

It was 10:06 when the second alarm came in.

We heard the third at 10:37 and the calm that had prevailed up until then was obscured by a tense, busy, silence as every man prepared himself for a really big one. I remember climbing the 101 year old spiral staircase telling myself that we had a good crew on tonight. That wasn't just blind reassurance, it was a good crew. I took the long staircase up to the third floor and put on some heavier clothes. There was a cold wind blowing out there. With an extra pair of socks in my back pocket, I checked for my hosestrap and spanner and then went down to wait with the rest of the men on the apparatus floor. All our gear was on the rig.

When the fourth alarm came in we were ready.

I was cold when we left quarters. Nervous cold. Every man in the crew was feeling that same chill and we remained silent as Bill Miller drove out. Our regular chauffeur, Vic Bengyak, was on vacation and I recall wishing that Bill was on the backstep with us. Every man was evaluating the crew, assuring himself that it was a competent one.

An entire group of stores was burning. It was a big one.

We reported to the chief in charge and were ordered into a bookstore on Broadway, between 22nd and 23rd Streets. I had the nozzle. Toby was behind me, followed by Joe Tringali. More reassurances.

When the Ladder Company forced the door open, we had our water and were to initiate an operation that we had executed many times before. We went in with two lines; Engine 24 to the right and 13 to the left. As we moved in together, 13 caught a large body of fire to her left. Straight ahead of us was the orange glow of still another body of fire. The heat was intense. There were obstacles in our path no matter where we turned—boxes of books, bookcases, and all sizes and shapes of debris.

Toby jumped onto a crate and I passed the line up to him just as 13's Lieutenant was yelling for his line. A wall to his left had dropped and, when it did, we discovered that the floor in the next store had collapsed.

Both companies were on top of it immediately, hitting the fire together, pouring water directly into the cellar. It had never occurred to any of us up until then that this fire, which was raging so fiercely all around us, was also burning right below us under the very floor we stood on. Suddenly, the Lieutenant was ordering us out. The floor near the doorway was getting soft and it didn't take us long, once we heard that, to get out. When our last man was out on the sidewalk, the entire floor that had supported us just seconds before gave way. An overwhelming sense of what could have been passed through me, accompanied by a deep feeling of relief.

There wasn't even time to talk about our close call. The spectators across Broadway were gasping in unison, and when we heard the ensuing shouts we directed our eyes upward. There were still companies scrambling to get off the roof of the doomed building and the fire was lapping dangerously close to the aerial ladder that was their only means of escape.

No one had to order us to open our lines. We shot water at a ninety degree angle up towards them, to shield them from the out-stretched hands of the blaze that was slapping at them persistantly. We held that stream steady until the last one of them was safely off the roof.

When the building came down, every company was engulfed in smoke and bombarded by debris. When it was all over, the outside walls stood firmly—a monument to something that no one was sure of yet.

MEN MISSING!

The fire had apparently burned itself out and we were all sure that the worst was over. But it was about then that the rumors started to circulate. Missing men! I don't know who, near us, first spoke those words, but I remember that we were all tight-lipped. Every one of us was outwardly rejecting the rumor, and inwardly praying that we were right—that the reports were false.

The head count seemed to take an eternity. When the results got back to us it was difficult to believe. There were twelve men unaccounted for.

Our company was all together and so was Engine 13. "Who's missing?" I was asking, as was every man at the scene who had heard the rumors. I wasn't even sure at that point exactly how many companies had responded to the alarm. There were finally whispers of some of the chiefs and their aides as possibilities. Then someone mentioned Ladder 7. I didn't want to believe any of the talk, but the next bit of news was even harder for me to believe. Someone said that they couldn't locate Engine 18. I can still hear my own voice insisting, "You guys better get your head count straight." There was no basis for my doubt, just pure obstinacy. I refused to believe what, by that time, everyone was sure of. I had just been with those men earlier in the evening. Their faces flashed vividly through my mind. I had contacted and spoken to them about that violation. They couldn't have just disappeared since then.

I released my breath in relief when I saw John Donovan of Engine 18 approaching us. We were all thinking the same thing. See, there's someone from 18. They must have been located. It was all a rotten mistake.

But then, as he came closer to where we stood, his face became visible. It was masked with horror. He was nearly incoherent when he spoke to us, trying desperately to relate what had just happened to him. He had been dangling; swaying over the inferno after the floor gave way. He was hanging onto the handle of the controlling nozzle by just three fingers. His rubber coat had started to burn and he was slipping, sure that there was no hope, when a hand reached out and grabbed the rescue loop on his Scott Airpak. Then there was another hand, and another. . . .

He had been the man who was sent out on my complaint, so he hadn't been with 18 when they responded to the alarm. He had gone with another company to search for them when they were reported missing.

Manny Fernandez, 18's regular chauffeur, appeared out of the night, and there was a lot of confusion as everyone started to ask questions. He had been changing when the alarm came in, and Jimmy Galanaugh had offered to drive.

Engine Company 18 and Ladder Company 7 had perished when that third alarm had come in, before we even arrived at the scene. There was no time to grasp that terrible fact because we were being ordered around the corner from where we had been operating.

When we turned the corner I, for one, could hardly believe my eyes. I just wasn't prepared for the sight before us. There was smoke and flames everywhere and we were sure that it was another 5th alarm of similar magnitude. But there, staring us in the face, was the same fire that we thought was extinguished.

SILENT PRAYER OFFERED

We were told to stand by until ordered to take our line into a haberdashery store. We waited, feeling the cold and dreading the fire.

As we stood by, we became increasingly aware of the commotion in front of the burned out drugstore. They were carrying out bodies. Two of them in body bags. I didn't know who they were. And I wondered, as we removed our helmets to say a silent prayer, if every man felt as sick as I did at that moment. Something that John McCole, a man in my company, had once said came back to me instantly. He had been referring to the Times Tower fire that he had been to a few years back, and the feeling he had when they carried out two dead firemen. "You'll never know how it feels until you see it with your own eyes."

I was feeling it then.

We were the next company to enter the building and, with the previous scene still fresh in our minds, I wasn't the only one who was experiencing a fear that was brand new.

We were to put a distributor to work in the haberdashery. It would enable us, we hoped, to pump a large volume of water into the fire below us through a hole that one of the ladder companies had chopped in the floor. Ladder 17 was working with us, but we hadn't even begun the operation when our Lieutenant was ordering us out. His judgment was sound, for as we backed away, about eight feet of the floor in front of us dropped like a bar of chocolate in one and two foot sections. We watched from the doorway as the semi-circle widened.

We asked the Chief if he could get a company to cut a hole in the floor near the door so we could at least get to some of the fire. "No, back away," he quickly replied. "That floor isn't safe. No one is to enter that store." One of the men asked the Chief if we could just walk over to the existing hole and drop a distributor into it. Again the Chief responded with a quick and firm 'no.' Just then, as if in affirmation of the Chief's decision, the entire floor collapsed into the cellar. The man who had suggested walking over to drop in the distributor looked slightly sick; his self-confidence suddenly gone. He was just thankful that he hadn't been allowed to take even a few steps toward that hole.

FIREFIGHTING GOES ON

We were relieved by another company for a few minutes, and the events of the evening were temporarily replaced in our minds by the hot coffee we were smelling and tasting. The damp cold night had penetrated my body to the bones, and I never appreciated a cup of coffee more in my life.

The Mayor was there, viewing the continuing disaster with a look of repressed anxiety on his face. And he was only seeing it from the sidewalk.

We were then sent into another section of the building.

We were to take our line up a staircase. The men who were coming down, as we were going up, warned us that the staircase was listing. We had advanced up two flights when the Chief in charge of the fire ordered us down. We could still see the fire raging at the top of the stairs and by this time we were striking at it in anger, hitting it from where we stood at the bottom of the stairs. That fire seemed like an enemy, more hated than any enemy in war or peace had ever been. It was as if it had taken on a distinct personality. We were frustrated at not being able to defeat it yet.

A LIFETIME'S EMOTIONS

We set up a multiversal nozzle, which develops a large calibre stream, and kept hitting it from below.

Another break. Hot broth this time. The cold that gnawed away at us was becoming almost as much of an enemy as the fire.

We were needed at the drugstore to assist in the search for bodies.

As we lowered the men of Ladder Company 24 into the gaping hole, their Lieutenant told us to be extremely careful. He immediately set about the task of inspecting a wall next to the area where we were working. After a careful examination, he found it to be sound and we continued on our grim assignment. By then we were suspicious of every last piece of material in the building. It was all heavy stuff, not just plaster board. However, all the officers on the scene were well aware of the dangers involved and were determined that there would be no further fatalities. They quietly and efficiently examined all the standing walls and beams, making sure that there would not be another collapse.

Toby was holding the rope as we lowered them down and we formed a chain, passing the debris along from the bottom until it found it's way onto the sidewalk outside. Fifteen minutes or so passed and we heard a rumbling sound. I thought that I was the only one who had heard it, but when I turned to ask the Lieutenant about it, I saw that he was returning from another area. He too had heard the noise and had immediately investigated it. It turned out to be just another company doing some drilling. We were reacting to our own fears.

Soon after that, one of the Chiefs gave the order for us to move out. We were being relieved.

I realized for the first time that it wasn't night anymore. Where had all those hours gone? Where is the fatigue I should be feeling? I had to get a call through to my wife. She must have heard about the fire on the news I thought, as we were leaving the building.

Suddenly I was completely captive to a strange, indescribable sentiment as I caught sight of the off-duty members of Engine Company 18 arriving at the scene. They had come, true to Fire Department tradition, to join in the search for their lost brothers. One thing was certain. No one would carry the bodies out but them.

It was the saddest, blackest night in the 101 year history of the New York City Fire Department, but I was experiencing a renewed pride in being a small part of what no one can deny is the greatest Fire Department in the world.

I had experienced an entire lifetime's worth of emotions in those hours. Panic, self-control, fear, relief, defeat, pride, all running into and over one another. Sadness and a sense of personal loss for real men I worked with and liked, and who were now just memories. Sorrow for their wives and children, and an undirected anger because twelve of them had to die to extinguish a fire. Love for a wife who was beside herself with worry, until I finally reached her by phone a short while ago, and for my children—my five year old daughter who asked if her daddy had died. I never realized that I could miss four kids so much.

The most distinct emotion—one that I'm experiencing still—is a true, undiluted awareness of living and breathing and being able to feel in so many different ways. Every second of that is sacred to me now. ▲

Thomas A. Reilly
Deputy Chief, 3rd Division

Walter J. Higgins
Battalion Chief, 7th Battalion

John J. Finley
Lieutenant, Ladder Co. 7

Joseph Priore
Lieutenant, 4th Battalion

James V. Galanaugh
Fr. 1st Grade, Engine Co. 18

Joseph Kelly (2)
Fr. 1st Grade, Engine Co. 18

Bernard A. Tepper
Fr. 1st Grade, Engine Co. 18

Daniel L. Rey
Prob. Fr., Engine Co. 18

William F. McCarron
Fr. 1st Grade, 3rd Division

Rudolph F. Kaminsky
Fr. 1st Grade, Ladder Co. 7

Carl Lee
Fr. 1st Grade, Ladder Co. 7

John G. Berry
Fr. 1st Grade, Ladder Co. 7

XXXXXXXXXXXXXXXXXXXXXXXXXXXXXXXXXXXXXXXXXXXXXXXXXXXXXXXXXXXXXXXXXXXXXXXXXX

WE REMEMBER

(Remarks of John J. O'Rourke, then Chief of Department, Memorial Day, October 8, 1986)

Almost twenty years have passed since the fateful day in 1966 when the New York Fire Department suffered the worst tragedy in its history. The calamitous occurance of Twenty-third Street will always be remembered by the members of this Department. The loss of twelve good men at one disastrous fire left a scar on our memories that can never really heal. The wound of that terrible night is still raw and painful in the mind of every firefighter present here today.

I was working as a Lieutenant in Brownsville that night when we learned of the collapse and the number of men trapped. As soon as we were relieved in the morning, we reported to the scene as a unit and offered our help in trying to locate our trapped members. I will never forget the look of sadness on the faces of the men who had worked all night, trying their best to bring the victims out alive. It was not to be. As the morning passed, hope grew dimmer and dimmer. Finally, we were ordered to assemble in the park across Twenty-third Street where a tearful Chief John O'Hagan told us the awful news that all of the victims had perished.

He thanked us all for coming to help and asked us to join him in prayer for the repose of their souls. As his successor, twice removed, I ask you to do the same. Not only for the twelve heroes of Twenty-third Street but for all our fallen brothers who have paid for their dedication with their most precious possession—their lives.

5-5-5-5

Box 598
October 17, 1966

Thomas A. Reilly
Deputy Chief, 3rd Division

Walter J. Higgins
Battalion Chief, 7th Battalion

John J. Finley
Lieutenant, Ladder Co. 7

Joseph Priore
Lieutenant, 4th Battalion

James V. Galanaugh
Fr. 1st Grade, Engine Co. 18

Joseph Kelly (2)
Fr. 1st Grade, Engine Co. 18

Bernard A. Tepper
Fr. 1st Grade, Engine Co. 18

Daniel L. Rey
Prob. Fr., Engine Co. 18

William F. McCarron
Fr. 1st Grade, 3rd Division

Rudloph F. Kaminsky
Fr. 1st Grade, Ladder Co. 7

Carl Lee
Fr. 1st Grade, Ladder Co. 7

John G. Berry
Fr, 1st Grade, Ladder Co. 7

FDNY Honor Roll at Fire Headquarters

Photo courtesy of FDNY

XXXXXXXXXXXXXXXXXXXXXXXXXXXXXXXXXXXXXXXXXXXXXXXXXXXXXXXXXXXXXXXXX

XXX

AFTERWORD

If you are considering a career in rescue work, you should know what qualities make for a good emergency worker. According to Dr. Mitchell of the ICISF, they are:

- - A caring attitude
- - A quick, intelligent mind
- - Leadership ability
- - An ability to function outside a career
- - Good support from family and friends
- - A flexible nature
- - An ability to handle everyday stress

Note that "a desire to make a lot of money" is **not** listed above. If money is your primary motivation, do yourself and the service a favor and seek another profession.

It is certainly true that rescue work and fire- fighting have negative aspects, but there is no greater feeling of self-worth and accomplishment than in knowing you helped save a life. So, if you should ever meet some insignificant boob who says, "Firemen do nothing but play cards and checkers," I hope you react by asking God to cure him of his ignorance. If you are a firefighter, you may want to punch his lights out; an act you may regret, but I wouldn't mind if you did.

XXXXXXXXXXXXXXXXXXXXXXXXXXXXXXXXXXXXXXXXXXXXXXXXXXXXXXXXXXXXXXX

xx

BIBLIOGRAPHY

Collapse of Burning Buildings, Vincent Dunn

FDNY Medal Day Book of 1991

FDNY Special Order No. 171, September 4, 1913

FIREHOUSE Magazine, September 1986

Maryland Rescue Journal, January 1984

The Bay News, 1979

The Chief, 1910

The Firemen's Herald, 1908

The New York Daily News, 1978, 1979, 1984

The New York Globe, 1908

The New York Times, 1978, 1991, 1993

The New York Post, 1978

The Tablet, 1978

UFA Fire Lines, August 1978

UFOA Trumpet, 1st qtr. of 1992

WNYF Magazine: Centennial issue of 1965

                        4th issue of 1966

                        4th issue of 1970

                        2nd issue of 1973

                        4th issue of 1976

                        3rd issue of 1978

                        4th issue of 1978

                        4th issue of 1986

                        2nd issue of 1990

xxxxxxxxxxxxxxxxxxxxxxxxxxxxxxxxxxxxxxxxxxxxxxxxxxxxxxxxxxxxxxxxxxxxxx

xx

APPENDIX

For information on Critical Incident Stress and a list of books and video tapes, contact:

International Critical Incident Stress Foundation (ICISF)
5018 Dorsey Hall Drive, Suite 104
Ellicott City, MD 21042
(410) 730-4311 or (410) 740-0065
Fax: (410) 730-4313

Also see page 144 for signs and symptoms of stress.

For FDNY members only:
For assistance in dealing with symptoms of stress,
call the Counseling Services Unit [CSU] at:
(212) 570-1693.
Contacting CSU is not subject to the chain of command
and all matters are kept strictly confidential.
If you doubt it, just try and get some information from
them that does not involve you personally.

For information about the New York Firefighters Burn Center Foundation, contact:

New York Firefighters Burn Center
c/o Ladder 61
21 Asch Loop
Bronx, New York 10475
(212) 379-1900 or (212) 860-9246

Fire service-related art work is available from the
Burn Center. Proceeds are used for burn prevention,
care and research.
See sample offerings on pages xiv and 24 by artist,
J. Capriano.
Quality prints are in full color.

xxxxxxxxxxxxxxxxxxxxxxxxxxxxxxxxxxxxxxxxxxxxxxxxxxxxxxxxxxxxxxxx

Other contributing artists:

Dave Hirsch
41 Union Square
Studio 1035
N.Y.C., NY 10003

John Goss
The Virgo Studio
P.O. Box 187
Forest Hills, NY 11375

Russ Poore, WNYF Graphics Unit. (Badge illustrations)

Fire service publications:

FIREHOUSE Magazine (monthly)
445 Broad Hollow Road
Melville, NY 11747
(516) 845-2700

WNYF Magazine (quarterly)
NYC Fire Academy
Randalls Island, NY 10035
(212) 860-9243

Recommended Reading:

"Collapse of Burning Buildings," Vincent Dunn

"Safety and Survival on the Fireground," V. Dunn

"Emergency Services Stress," Dr. Jeffrey T. Mitchell

*"23rd Street Fire ... as it happened," Frank Cull

**"The Firefighter's Cookbook," John Sineno

For an in-depth study of the worst loss in FDNY history, see this 8 page article in WNYF, 4th issue of 1976.

**Not only contains some outstanding recipes but also a short story of the joint effort between New York Hospital-Cornell Medical Center and NYC firefightersto establish a metropolitan area Burn Center. Sales of the book have raised a considerable amount of money for the NY FF Burn Center Foundation. Hopefully, this book will do the same.*

xxxxxxxxxxxxxxxxxxxxxxxxxxxxxxxxxxxxxxxxxxxxxxxxxxxxxxxxxxxxxxxxx

XXX

INDEX

XXXXXXXXXXXXXXXXXXXXXXXXXXXXXXXXXXXXXXXXXXXXXXXXXXXXXXXXXXXXXXXXX

XXX

XXX

XXX

XXX

ILLUSTRATIONS

XX

Comments and inquiries regarding any
part of this book are welcomed.

Address correspondence to:

Ernie DiMaria
c/o SUNSET Bookstore
P.O. Box 81024
Las Vegas, NV 89180

This book is available at special discount if used for fund
raising activities of any Volunteer Fire Department,
EMT/Paramedic Squad, Burn Center Foundation, or any other
organization devoted to Rescue Services.

For terms and conditions, write to SUNSET *Bookstore*.

XXXXXXXXXXXXXXXXXXXXXXXXXXXXXXXXXXXXXXXXXXXXXXXXXXXXXXXXXXXXXXXXXX